IN
OF CLAY

A BOOK OF MEDITATIONS

Blessings,
Marcia Schwartz

IN JARS OF CLAY

A BOOK OF MEDITATIONS

MARCIA SCHWARTZ
ILLUSTRATIONS BY TOOTIE EBEL

outskirtspress
DENVER, COLORADO

Outskirts Press, Inc.
http://www.outskirtspress.com

ISBN: 978-1-4787-0755-4

Outskirts Press and the "OP" logo are trademarks belonging to Outskirts Press, Inc.

PRINTED IN THE UNITED STATES OF AMERICA

Acknowledgments

All Scripture quotations, unless otherwise indicated, are taken from from the Holy Bible, New International Version ®, Copyright ©1973, 1978, 1984, 2011 by Biblica, Inc.TM Used by permission of Zondervan. All rights reserved worldwide, www.zondervan.com.

Scripture taken from "The Message," by Eugene H. Peterson, copyright date 1993, 1994, 1995, Nav Press Publishing Group. Used by permission of Nav Press, All Rights Reserved. www.navpress.com. (1-800-366-7788)

Scripture quotations marked (NLT) are taken from the Holy Bible, New Living translation, Copyright © 1996, 2004, 2007 by the Tyndale House Foundation. Used by permission of Tyndale House Publishers, Inc., Carol Stream, Illinois 60188. All rights reserved.

Scripture quotations from "The Living Bible," Copyright © 1971 by Tyndale House Publishers, Wheaton, Illinois 60187. All rights reserved.

Scriptures marked KJV are from the King James Version of the Bible.

And I said to the man who stood at the gate of the year:
"Give me a light that I may tread safely into the unknown!"

And he said: "Go out into the darkness and put your hand
into the hand of God. That should be to you better than
light and safer than a known way."

— Minnie Louise Haskins

The steadfast love of God never ceases, His mercies nev-
er come to an end; they are new every morning; great is
Thy faithfulness. "The Lord is My portion," says my soul,
"therefore I will hope in Him."

—Lamentations 3:22-24

Contents

1

In Jars of Clay

2 Cor. 4:7 But we have this treasure in jars of clay to show that this all-surpassing power is from God and not from us.

A dodo was a heavy-breasted, waddling bird related to pigeons and doves, and first described for us by the Dutch explorers who landed on the East Indies isle of Mauritius. This species of bird is now extinct from the earth. The Dutch settlers brought pigs to Mauritius which were a big factor in dodo extinction by the mid-to-late 1600's. Deforestation may have also contributed because the poor, flightless bird couldn't hide from its predators.

The Dutch sailors ridiculed the guileless, long-beaked bird which seemed too dumb to escape by calling it a "dodo." Lewis Carroll contributed a lasting image of the dodo by making it a character in his children's book, "Alice In Wonderland."

In many ways, the dodo's body was as vulnerable and fragile as ours. The flightless bird was powerless to flee its predators. We, too, have temporal bodies made from dirt–or clay, as termed by St. Paul in Second Corinthians. Our bodies are as corruptible and common as a clay pot. EXCEPT– as Christians, our jars are filled with a great treasure– the glory of God in Christ Jesus our Savior! God "made His light to shine in our hearts to give us the light of the knowledge of the glory of God in the face of Christ." (2 Cor. 4:6)

God has put into our bodies the imperishable through the death and Resurrection of his Son. We are not flightless, but heaven-bound through His Spirit which bears us up. We shall never become extinct as long as we carry within us the precious treasure of the Gospel.

"Dumb as a dodo" –absolutely not! For our jars radiate the saving Gospel light which is Christ in our hearts!

Prayer: Glory to You, Lord God, for sending Your Son to rescue us from sin and death. Praise to You for Your light which shines through our jars of clay. Amen.

2

The Cedars of Lebanon

2 Cor. 2:14 But thanks be to God, who always leads us in triumphal procession in Christ and through us spreads everywhere the fragrance of the knowledge of him.

Most magnificent among the trees referred to in the Old Testament were those tall, beautiful and aromatic cedars towering from the hillsides of Lebanon. Their wood was highly prized because it was so strong and straight, a prime resource for building pillars and masts, temples and ships. Trade was vigorous for the ancient Phoenicians for their precious cedars were always in demand. Because the cedar forests have been so ravaged through the ages, there are very few of the glorious trees remaining there today.

The value of cedars to the ancients was very apparent in I Chronicles 17:1. David was settled in his new domicile when he said to Nathan the prophet, "Here I am living in a palace of cedar, while the ark of the covenant of the Lord is under a tent." The Lord subsequently informed David that He didn't want him to build His temple; that task/honor would fall upon David's son, Solomon. When the days were accomplished that Solomon should begin, he contacted Hiram, king of Tyre, and put in his order for wood. "Send me cedar logs as you did for my father David when you sent him cedar to build a palace to live in. Now I am about to build a temple for the Name of the Lord my God..." (2 Chron. 2:3-4)

Truly the cedars of Lebanon were the trees of kings. Can you imagine what it must have been like to stand under the beams and rafters of their edifices, inhaling the intoxicating sweetness of the aromatic wood? If our churches today were filled with such delight for the olfactory senses, perhaps people would flock to them every time their doors were opened.

But actually, they do emanate with something far more precious: the One who loved us and died for us, "a fragrant offering and sacrifice to God." (Eph. 5:1&2)

As we process into our churches, whether they are humble or grand, they are infused with a fragrance far greater than that exuded by whole forests of cedars of Lebanon. They are infused with the sweet, sweet fragrance of Christ!

Prayer: Dear Immaculate Jesus, forgive us our sins—make us righteous in You, and wherever we go today, and whatever we do and say, may we trail the fragrance of You. Amen.

3

Jethro's Advice on Handling Stress

Read Exodus 18

Exodus 18:14, 18b (NLT) When his father-in-law saw all that Moses was doing for the people, he said, "What is this you are doing for the people? Why do you alone sit as a judge, while all these people stand around you from morning till evening?".... "The work is too heavy for you; you cannot handle it alone."

Moses must have been about ready to pull his hair out! He had been working from sun-up to sun-down sitting as a judge for the Israelite people. They stood around him in great numbers, needing him to settle many matters using God's decrees and laws.

Moses's father-in-law, Jethro, came to visit him in the desert, and was immediately concerned about the stress and strain this routine was putting on Moses. In essence, Jethro said, "My son, this is not good for you! Let me give you some advice. Select some of the more capable and trustworthy men and delegate them to help you carry the load. You take the difficult cases and leave the simpler cases to them. That will make your load lighter." And then as written in the NIV translation of Exodus: "you will be able to stand the strain, and all these people will go home satisfied." (Ex. 18:22b & 23b)

Moses took Jethro's inspired advice and adopted some priorities. He decided what should be his responsibilities and then appointed leaders and organized their sphere of duty so that they became "officials over thousand, hundreds, fifties and tens." (Ex. 18:25b) This more efficient organization of the people surely reduced the headaches of Moses and gave him more time for physical and spiritual renewal.

Henry David Thoreau's advice many generations later seems to mirror Jethro's. The 18th century New England philosopher espoused: "Our life is frittered away by detail. Simplify, simplify, simplify! I say let your affairs be as two or three, and not a hundred or a thousand..."

We can apply the wisdom of Jethro and Thoreau to our own lives as we analyze our daily routines. Are there a few things which are important and should be given priority, and others which could be sacrificed or simplified? Could we delegate certain tasks to other members of the household or could we collaborate with a friend? Are there ways to de-clutter, not only our workplaces, but our lives, and regenerate our souls by spending more time with God, with nature, with hobbies, and with our loved ones?

Will we listen to the advice of others, set priorities, delegate, organize, and *simplify* so that our lives will be less stressful?

Prayer: Dear Father in heaven who manages a universe, give us wisdom as we manage our lives, and may You always be given our number one priority. We seek healthy lives relieved of stress and strain and lived to Your glory. Amen.

4

Empty Church Pews

Eph. 2:19 So then you are no longer strangers and aliens, but you are fellow citizens with the saints and members of the household of God. (ESV)

There are certain scenes in old movies that grab the imagination and live in the mind long after the credits roll and the curtain comes down. One of those that lingers for me is the last scene of "Places of the Heart." Sally Fields plays Edna Spaulding, a gritty widow who faces farm foreclosure after her sheriff husband is killed during the Depression. With the help of a black man and a blind man, she plants a cotton crop on her Texas land, hoping to make enough money to stave off the loss of her home to the bank. After a series of set-backs including interference by the Ku Klux Klan, tornadoes, and other disasters, Edna and the two men bring in a crop in the nick of time. In a sad parting, the black man finds it necessary to leave the farm.

In the last scene of the movie, Edna and her two children are seated in church. The communion plate is being passed when, with the magic of screen cinema, her dead husband appears at her side, and the half-empty pews fill up with the other people, some deceased and some from among the living, black and white, friends and family, as together they share a reunion of their souls in Holy Communion.

Church pews in rural areas are so empty these days. Many of the younger people have moved to the cities for their jobs and other benefits, and many of the older members have left these earthly portals. In my own church, the pews were once packed with families and now they are disturbingly empty. Sometimes, I like to envision all the former parishioners sitting among us still. Cornelius, the bearded organist who dressed like Buffalo Bill; Mrs. Schnutte, the meticulous director of the altar guild; Nell, who led the Missionary Circle with such aplomb; Orville, the pipe-smoking, ever-faithful elder; and Lydia, the choir member with the sweet soprano voice– all these and so many more once populated our church. In my vision, we are all together again, the seen and the unseen, united "saints and members of the household of God." (See Eph. 2:19 above) With all our flaws and failings, our hearts were, and still are, bound in a united love for God. The last lines of the Apostle's Creed echo from pew to pew as we avow once more: "I believe in the Holy Spirit, the holy Christian Church, **the communion of saints**, the forgiveness of sins, the resurrection of the body, and the life everlasting. Amen."

Prayer: Jesus Christ, Bridegroom of the Church, You are the blessed tie that binds our hearts in Christian love and mystic communion. As brothers and sisters in Christ, help us to be forgiving and loving of each other. We thank and praise You for making us fellow members of the household of God. Amen.

5

Gospel in My Pocket

Mark 16:15 Go into all the world and preach the Good News to everyone, everywhere. (NLT)

When my little brother was in kindergarten he brought home his first packet of individual school pictures. My mother carefully cut the sheet of photos apart, and put twenty of them in the pocket of Jerry's jacket and sent them back to school with him the next day.

When he arrived home that afternoon, my mother was curious to see how many of his little classmates he had traded with at school that day. She pulled the photos from his pocket, but not one of them was of another child– all twenty photos of Jerry came home with him.

"Why didn't you trade with someone?" my mother asked him.

"I looked at some of the others, but mine were the best so I just decided to keep them," he soberly replied. I don't remember whether we were ever able to convince him to trade or give away any of his twenty pictures.

Are we sometimes like a little boy who keeps the precious contents of his pocket to himself? We carry around with us a beautiful picture of Salvation– the Good News– the Gospel!

But do we hold it close to the vest, reluctant for a variety of reasons to share it? Meanwhile, we carry that Gospel in our pockets, every blessed bit of it.

Someday we'll go home from the schoolroom of our earthly existence and our Father will ask, "Did you give away the contents of your pocket– did you tell others how much I love them, and how much I want them in heaven, too? My precious child, I love you, and I trusted you with a sacred mission of spreading the gospel. Did you share it?"

Prayer: Dear Father God, thank you for the Good News that we have been rescued from our sins by the death and resurrection of Jesus who paid the price for us. It's just too good of news not to share it. By your Holy Spirit, show us how, and lead us in ways to do it. Amen.

6

The Lighted Cross on Highway 73

John 1:4, 5a In him was life, and that life was the light of men. The light shines in the darkness....

A landmark in our community has been the lighted cross affixed to the steeple of a rural church about four miles north of our town. Beyond the church, one rounds a large downhill bend in the road and then has a short, straight shot south into Falls City. Travelers coming in the dark from the west could see the cross from miles away before a short in the wiring caused a fire which damaged the church and extinguished the cross.

After many months of darkness, the cross was repaired, much to the approval of many people in our community. I recall one time in particular when the glowing landmark had been a godsend. My husband and I were driving home on a snowy evening. As we crept slowly down the highway, nearly all we could see from the car windows were blowing curtains of white. The wipers kept plowing away the snow which piled like cotton batting against the windshield. We were tense and apprehensive as we motored slowly through the darkness, snow crunching under our wheels. And then, at last, we topped a hill, and far ahead like a beacon guiding us to shore, we saw the lighted cross on St. Paul's church. With a sigh of relief, we knew we were almost home.

Through the years, friends and neighbors have also testified to a sense of comfort and certainty as they traveled that road and looked toward the lighted cross on the horizon. If one lost his bearings, he was set aright when the cross appeared out of the darkness. It was also a signpost when giving directions to others who weren't familiar with the area. I'm glad the good parishioners of St. Paul's decided to repair the stricken cross for it had been missed.

But the most important cross of all is the one on which Jesus actually sacrificed his life for our sins. Yes, the cross of Christ still shines out into the darkness of this world, and unlike the electric one on the church north of town, nothing shall ever put out its light. The cross on which he died glows eternally with His victory over sin and death. We need to keep our eyes upon Jesus as we travel through this dark wilderness, and one day, He will lead us around the bend, down the hill, and safely home!

Prayer: Dear Lord Jesus, our Light and our Salvation, help us to keep our eyes on You as we trust You to lead us safely to our heavenly home. Amen.

7

Waiting on the Lord

Lam. 3: 22-24 Because of the Lord's great love we are not consumed, for his compassions never fail. They are new every morning; great is thy faithfulness. I say to myself, "The Lord is my portion; therefore I will wait on him."

In the days of Caesar Augustus there was a devout Jew named Simeon who had been promised by God that he would not die until he saw the long-awaited Messiah. We can imagine how the old gray-bearded man looked, day after day, shuffling to the temple to pray and watch for the baby who would become the Redeemer of the human race. And isn't it amazing that on the day that Mary and Joseph brought the infant Jesus to the Temple to present Him to the Lord, that Simeon recognized Him immediately!

How his weary old heart must have rejoiced, and how his wrinkled old fingers must have reached out in wonder and awe to touch the Savior of the World, our Emmanuel. He praised God saying, "For my eyes have seen your salvation." (Luke 2:30) "Let now your servant depart in peace." (Luke 2:29b)

We don't have to wait for the arrival of the Messiah, for that promise has been fulfilled in Bethlehem over two thousand years ago. But we also are waiting on another promise made by God, and that is the *second* coming of our Lord. The first coming was as a baby in a lowly manger, born of a virgin. This next time He will come in the clouds with great glory! "At that time the sign of the Son of Man will appear in the sky, and all the nations of the earth will mourn. They will see the Son of Man coming on the clouds of the sky, with power and great glory." (Matt. 24:30) There are several other references in the New Testament as to His coming on the clouds, including Acts 1:9-11 and Mark 13:26.

Simeon is a great example to us to wait patiently upon the Lord. Like him we must remain steadfast, abounding in hope, knowing that God always fulfils his promises. Whoever remains among the living on that wondrous day when Jesus parts the clouds and arrives on earth again, will behold the glorious Second Coming of the Messiah. The words of the Psalmist seem to apply to both the first and second coming: "I am confident of this: I will see the goodness of the Lord in the land of the living. Wait for the Lord; be strong and take heart and wait for the Lord." (Ps. 27:13,14)

Prayer: Wonderful Counselor, Mighty God, Everlasting Father, Prince of Peace, we celebrate each year Your first coming with glad Christmas carols and loud hosannas. How wonderful that You came to rescue us from our sins! Now we wait for Your Second Coming with eager antici- pation. Amen.

8

Treasure Hunt

Matt. 13:44 The kingdom of heaven is like treasure hidden in a field. When a man found it, he hid it again, and then in his joy went and sold all he had and bought the field.

"Geocaching" has really been catching on in the last decade or so. To play this high-tech treasure-hunting game you will need a GPS device or a smart-phone to search out hidden trinkets using co-ordinates supplied by a website. When you find the cache box, there will be a logbook where you can sign in, and if you choose to take the small item stored there, you are obligated to leave something else behind.

Last summer we met a couple at a Nebraska park who kept circling willy-nilly around a footbridge. We asked if we could be of assistance and learned that they had driven hundreds of miles from Kansas to mark off another stash on their geocaching map. The hobby kept them busy scouting out sites all over the Midwest. They found the box under a bush nearby and opened it to find a toy action figure.

Jesus related a parable in Matthew 13 about a man who found a treasure hidden in a field– a treasure so priceless that he exchanged everything he had to obtain it. The treasure was the Kingdom of God. Right on the heels of this parable, Jesus told another which relates to it:

"Again, the kingdom of heaven is like a merchant looking for fine pearls. When he found one of great value, he went away and sold everything he had and bought it." (Matt. 13:45)

In a sense, we are all out geocaching. We are searching for the treasures of existence, and looking for fulfilment for our souls. We run hither and yon, trying new experiences, new hobbies, new pleasures to fulfil inexplicable longings. I think in these two parables above, Jesus is leading us to give up the trivial pursuits, the games, and trinkets to obtain something of far greater value– the kingdom of heaven!

Whether we "geocachers" realize it or not, we "hunger and thirst" for meaning in our lives, and lasting fulfilment. We want to check in on the logbook of heaven and know that we have indeed found the huge, glowing priceless pearl of existence, and we want to tell others where they, too, can find it for themselves. We need to leave in the cache box the guidebook, the map, the co-ordinates to heaven– the Bible. And then instead of running around "willy-nilly," we will find the true treasure, for the Bible tells us… "seek ye first the kingdom of God, and his righteousness; and all these things shall be added unto you." (Matt. 6:33 KJV)

Prayer: O, Dear Jesus, thank you for the wonderful treasures you have provided for us in Your Scriptures. Thank you for Your precious parables which direct us to the kingdom of heaven! Keep us from ever getting lost from You, and help us to plant Bibles all over the world! Amen.

9

The Sword of the Spirit

Eph. 6:17 Take the helmet of salvation and the sword of the Spirit, which is the word of God.

Ps. 119:11a I have hidden your word in my heart.....

"Why do I have to memorize all these Bible verses?" asked the student preparing for his Confirmation. That disgruntled young man may one day find himself in circumstances where God's Word buried in his heart will be his strength and sustenance. For instance, many prisoners of war have been able to endure horrific conditions because of Scripture hidden in their hearts.

Commander Howard Rutledge was a Navy pilot who was shot down and taken prisoner during the early days of the Vietnam war. He wrote about his seven long years of imprisonment in his book, "In the Presence of Mine Enemies" (Fleming H. Revell, 1973). Howard was strengthened to endure torture and shackles in the notorious Hanoi Hilton by recalling Scriptures and gospel songs he had learned as a youngster. During his military years he had fallen away from the church, but trapped in the heat, filth, hunger, dysentery, vermin (huge rats and spiders as big as a fist) and loneliness of solitary confinement, he found solace in God's Word.

"How I struggled to recall those Scriptures and hymns! I was amazed at how much I could recall; regrettably, I had not seen the importance of memorizing verses from the Bible or learning gospel songs (when I was young). Now when I needed them, it was too late. I never dreamed thinking about one memorized verse could have made a whole day bearable....How often I wished I had really worked to hide God's Word in my heart." ("In the Presence of Mine Enemies," pg. 32)

The prisoners devised a code, tapping out messages through the concrete walls, and in this way shared whatever Scripture each could recall, and together they compiled a resource of help and hope. Howard vowed that if he ever made it out of the prison he would join his family's church and become the spiritual head of his family. A vow he was finally able to keep when he was released from prison in February, 1973, and was joyfully reunited with his family who for many years didn't even know if he was alive.

Though we may never be a POW, we may find ourselves imprisoned in other ways, and the Word we have hid in our hearts will be invaluable in seeing us through. Whether in a hospital bed, a nursing home, or suffering in a myriad of ways, the mighty sword of God's Word will guard and protect our spirits during the turmoil of this life.

Prayer: O Faithful Lord, how wonderful the way You work through Your Word to strengthen our faith! Thank You for men like Howard Rutledge who remind us how important it is to memorize, learn, and meditate on Your Word. Amen.

10

Under the Stars

Ps. 19:1 The heavens declare the glory of God; And the firmament shows His handiwork. (NKJV)

When I heard the Learn'd Astronomer
When the proofs, the figures, were ranged in columns before me;
When I was shown the charts and diagrams,
to add, divide and measure them;
When I, sitting, heard the astronomer,
where he lectured with much applause in the lecture room,
How soon, unaccountable, I became tired and sick;
Till rising and gliding out, I wander'd off by myself,
In the mystical moist night-air, and from time to time,
Look'd up in perfect silence at the stars.

–from "Leaves of Grass" by Walt Whitman

Have you ever sat through a very boring lecture, perhaps a "Power-Point" one with all kinds of charts and diagrams, figures and formulas? Walt Whitman, a venerable voice in American poetry, attended a lecture presented by a highly educated astronomer, but became "tired and sick" of it, got up and slipped out into the "mystical, moist night-air" where he "look'd up in perfect silence at the stars." Being out under a velvet sky in the sweet, earthy air and wandering under a canopy of stars was profoundly more satisfying to him, and the silence spoke volumes more than the noisy, stuffy lecture room. How much more satisfying it is to "experience" nature than to just dissect it in scientific ways! (Tasting ice cream is far better than all the explanations of it in the world!)

There's no denying that intellectual investigation produces marvelous inventions and rewards, and perhaps a better understanding of the universe. However, in this information- cluttered world we sometimes need to pause and consider the "Power-Point" presentations which unfold over our heads and under our feet.

Poetry often "cuts to the core" of things more adroitly than a college textbook. The book of Job in the Old Testament is a masterful work of poetry in which puny men try to understand the ways of God, pontificating about the reasons for suffering, etc., in the small lecture rooms of their minds. At last the Lord speaks to Job and asks many questions about Job's right and ability to ever know His Mind. One subject was the stars: "Can you bind the beautiful Pleiades? (Or the *twinkling* Pleiades) Can you loose the cords of Orion? Can you bring forth the constellations in their season (or *the morning star in its season*) or lead out the Bear with its cubs?" (Job 38: 31 &32, with italicized words from the footnotes in the NIV translation)

God does not have to explain or justify anything for His ways are light-years beyond the understanding of Job and his friends....or you or me. Ours is not to manufacture the stars or the galaxies, or keep them in their places in the firmament; ours is but to praise the God who made them.

Prayer: Our Holy, Amazing, Omnipotent God, Your ways are far beyond our understanding, but we praise You for giving us the capacity to simply stand in awe under Your stars and breathe in the wonders of the universe. Amen.

11

Snapshots of Two Fathers

Psalms 127:3 Sons are a heritage from the Lord, children a reward from him.

High on the neighbor's roof in a fine, crisp October morning, I saw a roofer and his three sons putting on new shingles. The breeze wisped their blond hair from stocking caps and sweatshirt hoods. The three boys, between ten and sixteen years of age, maneuvered agilely in sneakers about the roof, sometimes boosting themselves along in a sitting position on well-patched jeans.

The oldest boy lined up the shingles, deftly placed a nail from his apron and with several sharp blows of the hammer anchored it into place. The second boy carried shingles to his father who cut them with swift precision and drilled them to the roof with a hammer-gun. The smallest boy scooted up and down the ladder gathering up scraps on the roof and in the yard below, his white sweatshirt striking as a dove against the blue sky and lofty green of the neighboring pines.

In an age when families seem to often fall apart and the apprenticeship of son to father in learning a trade is outmoded; when manual labor is scorned, and some young people don't know the meaning of work, that strong young father and his progeny was a beguiling snapshot of what a father and his sons could be!

Then in November I saw another father playing football with his two sons. "Keep your eyes on the ball and keep running," shouted the father who spiraled the brown pigskin towards a third grade boy who caught the ball with a shriek and bounded away from a smaller boy who plodded along behind. "Let's tackle Dad," the older boy said and soon all three landed giggling and shouting in a pile of autumn leaves. This time the snapshot was of a father and his sons at play– such a simple and natural thing, but so important to stability, well-being, and happiness.

I happen to know that, most importantly, both those fathers are seated with their sons in the church pews every Sunday, setting an example, guiding their spiritual development, giving them strong Christian roots.

A father who teaches his children, plays with his children, and guides them in things of the Spirit is one who cherishes them as a reward from God. And those children are going to more easily trust and love a Heavenly Father because they trust and love an earthly one. There is no higher calling for a man, and none more beautiful.

Prayer: Our Father who art in heaven, thank you for creating families for the nurture of the young. Impress upon fathers everywhere the crucial importance of their role, and help them to love their children and nurture them well. Amen.

12

"Got Milk"

I Peter 2:2 Like newborn babies, crave pure spiritual milk, so that by it you may grow up in your salvation.

Hebrews 5:12 In fact, though by this time you ought to be teachers, you need someone to teach you the elementary truths of God's word all over again. You need milk, not solid food! Anyone who lives on milk, being still an infant, is not acquainted with the teaching about righteousness.

Celebrities sporting milk mustaches are the hallmarks of a successful ad campaign sponsored by the California Milk Processors Board. Surely most of us are familiar with many of the movie stars, athletes, and other role models who display their fit bodies and white-wreathed smiles.

"Body by milk" the full-color ads proclaim as they sell us on the healthy benefits of this first and basic food. Strong bones from its calcium, good muscles from its protein, milk is full of nutrition. After all, Michael Jordan and Christie Brinkley drink it!

The benefits of "spiritual milk" are proclaimed in the Bible by Peter who urges us to "crave"milk like a newborn baby–seek its life-giving benefit. St. Paul, though, addresses older

Christians who should be growing beyond babyhood and eating "solid" food. In a letter to the Hebrews, he scolds a group of early Christians who had been trained in Christianity but were forgetting elemental principles, and were going backward instead of forward in the faith. "The Message" rendering of the Bible puts it bluntly in Hebrews 6: "So come on, let's leave the preschool fingerpainting exercises on Christ and get on with the grand work of art. Grow up in Christ."

But how do we grow up in Christ? We've "got milk" and now it's time to dig deeper.

We must challenge our minds and spirits by earnest study of God's Word, make time for Bible study and prayer, meet with others who are also attempting to go beyond the basics and become mature Christians. We need to become more attuned to the will of God and more fit for service.

We have known young people and older ones, too, who have been instructed in the faith, perhaps been baptized and confirmed and then "drop out" instead of continuing to learn and go forward. To nurture our faith and relationship to God, we all need to "Grow in the grace and knowledge of our Lord and Savior Jesus Christ." (2 Peter 3:18a)

With God's help, my mantra for this new year will be to "dig deeper!"

Prayer: Dear Lord God, thank you for those who have schooled us in the Word and who are role models in the faith. Thank you for the "milk" and now nurture us with "solid food" so we will grow and mature in You. Amen.

13

Savior, Fill My Cup

John 4:14 But whosoever drinketh of the water that I shall give him shall never thirst; but the water that I shall give him shall be a well of water springing up into everlasting life. (KJV)

A mother was careful not to fill her toddler's cup to the top in case the child's young and inexperienced hands might spill the contents. But the child wasn't happy with half a cup of juice.

She pointed to the rim of the cup with a chubby little finger and said, "Fill it to here, Mama; fill it all the way up."

Can't we all relate to that little girl? When we are thirsty, we are really thirsty, and we want a good long drink. I've read of people dehydrated and stumbling through the desert who would give everything they owned for one drink of water. How good a frosty glass of iced tea tastes when we are relaxing after working in the sun! Liquid refreshment keeps us from dehydrating, and this most basic of all needs drives us continually to be filled.

Jesus was hot and tired after a long journey on foot when he neared Jacob's well in Samaria. A Samaritan woman with a somewhat shady past came to draw water. Jesus asked her, "Will you give me a drink?" (John 4:7) She was shocked that a Jew would even speak to her as Jews felt that Samaritans were unclean and to be avoided. Jesus says in so many words, "Woman, if you knew who I am, you would ask, and I would give you living water so that you will never thirst again." Of course, he was speaking of spiritual water for her soul. She went to the well for H2O that day, but instead she found the Messiah!

Richard Blanchard, a Methodist pastor, wrote the beloved song, "Fill My Cup, Lord," in 1964. It became the number one gospel song during the 1970's. In his personal life, Richard Blanchard had many struggles including health problems and the tragic accident in which his son became a quadriplegic at age 17. However, music was always an important part of his ministry which included writing hymns. He claims the words to "Fill My Cup, Lord" were inspired by God, and came to him in a rush of about six minutes. The Samaritan woman at the well could certainly have joined him in singing: "Fill my cup Lord, I lift it up, Lord! Come and quench this thirsting soul. Bread of heaven, feed me till I want no more. Fill my cup, fill it up and make me whole."

When we are thirsty and need to drink from His Spirit, how wonderful that all we have to do is ask!

Prayer: Dear Lord of Living Water, sometimes we are weak and heavy-laden with the cares of this world. Sometimes we are so caught up in the carnal that we don't even realize there's a spiritual need that isn't being filled. Gently, offer again to fill our cups. Amen.

14

To Tattoo or Not To

Leviticus 19:28a Do not cut your bodies for the dead or put tattoo marks on yourselves...

Galations 3:25 Now that faith has come, we are no longer under the supervision of the law.

A pastor in Michigan has opened a tattoo parlor inside his church in an effort to reach people who wouldn't ordinarily venture inside a traditional church. When I read the article about this in the newspaper (Jan. 2012), I could just imagine the range of reactions to the Serenity Tattoo Parlor. They probably ranged from "Hosanna!" to "Holy Smokes!"

A tattoo parlor in church! I wonder– what would Jesus think? Researching the subject of Christianity and "skin art," I found some adamant stands taken against it based on Levitical law (Lev. 19:28, as written above). Tattooing, along with other customs of the pagans was forbidden by God as he called his people to come out from among the heathens. It seems that tattooing, though it is becoming more popular by leaps and bounds in modern America, is really a very old practice going back into antiquity.

Tattooing is taboo for some Christians because they believe that it is defiling the body, "the temple of God." (See I Cor. 6:19

and I Cor. 3:16-17) However, our sacred bodies can also be defiled by overeating, over-drinking, stressing our hearts, piercing our ears or noses, etc.

There are also practical reasons to resist "inking up." By law, minors in most states will need permission by a parent or caretaker. One should be aware of risks such as hepatitis, skin infection, future detriment in job-seeking, and the real possibility of getting tired of it.

Removing tattoos by laser is very painful and costly; some dermatologists charge thousands of dollars for removal and insurance doesn't cover it.

Those Christians who accept the practice of tattooing are ones who believe that we are no longer bound to Levitical law. (See Gal. 3:25 above) Some of these New Testament Christians remind us that Jesus, himself, ate with sinners and walked among them for the purpose of bringing them into the fold. Whether Jesus would approve of such an outlandish thing as a tattoo parlor in church, I do not know.

What I do know is that we Believers already bear a tattoo which shows that we belong to Christ, "written not with ink but with the Spirit of the living God, not on tablets of stone but on tablets of human hearts." (2 Cor. 3:3b)

God has already put his seal (tattoo) upon us!

Prayer: Our Risen Savior, You bear the scars on Your hands and feet which disfigured You so that You could secure our eternal salvation. How precious are those marks showing Your great love for us! How we praise and thank You! Amen.

15

The Hominy War

Luke 6:36 You must be compassionate, just as your Father is compassionate. (NLT)

Matt. 5:9 Blessed are the peacemakers; for they shall be called the children of God.

My five-year-old brother hated hominy! Those big, white chewy kernels of maize stuck in his craw like globs of glue. But my grandmother Iva believed that children should clean their plates; and as a depression-era survivor, she also could not abide throwing away good food.

My younger brother and sister and I were staying with Grandma while Mom was in the hospital with a new baby.

"Now you eat that hominy, young man, before you can leave this table!" she commanded.

My stubborn little brother crossed his arms and reared against the chair back, holding his tightly closed lips in a firm-lined resistance.

After an awkward standoff of ten minutes or more, my sister, age six, said to our grandmother in her most respectful "peacemaker" voice, "Grandma, would it help if I ate his hominy for him?"

I don't remember how her offer was received, but I've always been slightly in awe of my sister's compassion for her little brother and her desire to appease Grandma.

The Bible verse from Luke 6 quoted above says that we *must* have compassion on others.

If we are truly Godly, we will care for the plight of those around us. Jesus was compassionate on the hungry crowds, the weak, the sick, the dying. I wonder if He might even have offered to eat that hominy to redeem a brother and end a standoff!

There are so many people in the world who are deserving of our compassion; those who suffer as a result of earthquakes, floods, tornadoes, famine and wars. Many are destitute, homeless, hungry, and in need of our prayers, our emissaries, and our dollars. We *must* have compassion upon them if we would emulate Jesus.

"Compassion" and "peacemaking" seem to me to be related, for they both grow out of the root of "Caring." We will be called "the children of God" when in mercy we apply ourselves to brokering peace, just as my little sister did those many nights ago in our grandma's kitchen.

Prayer: Our merciful Jesus, help us to not only "talk the talk" but to "walk the walk" as we reach out to others with caring hearts; and everlasting thanks be unto You for Your compassion on us that took You to the cross! Amen.

16

The Midas Touch

Ps. 52:7a Here now is the man who did not make God his stronghold but trusted in his great wealth.

King Midas was a character in mythology who was rewarded for a kindness by being allowed one wish from the god Dionysus. As one not given to deep thought, Midas just popped a wish off the top of his head. He asked that everything he touched would turn to gold!

Soon he learned that he should have thought things through better. His food turned to gold when it touched his lips and he grew very thin. His bed turned into an uncomfortable cold, hard slab of solid gold. Thus he learned that he dared not touch his beloved little daughter or she, too, would succumb to the curse. One day, she came running to him, and in an off-guard moment, he reached out to stroke her hair, then drew his hand back in alarm as he felt only briefly its softness. Alas, it was too late–she turned into a golden statue.

The king regretted his greedy request and implored Dionysus to reverse the wish. The god took pity on Midas and granted the second wish, but Midas ended up even poorer than he had been before, in material goods, that is; but as he hugged his little flesh and blood daughter, he realized that he was rich in the things of real value.

Every once in a while we read of non-mythical people who have found that great wealth holds them back from finding a satisfying way of life. One such person was Tom Shadyac, an A-list Hollywood director who had accumulated a fortune directing blockbuster comedy movies.

After a bicycle wreck in 2007 nearly cost him his life, he began a journey of the soul that ended with him giving away most of his wealth to good causes and moving from his mansion into a trailer house in Malibu. He eventually produced a documentary movie (2011) entitled "I Am," which explores the interconnectedness of humans, and the idea, "am I not my brother's keeper?"

Tom Shadyac had been the King Midas of Hollywood; every movie he touched turned to gold at the box office, and yet it did not satisfy his soul. He found it too difficult to manage the stifling wealth and yet continue on his new life's journey, so he unloaded it. This is not to say that one mold fits all. J. C. Penney was a man who was able to maintain his wealth and use it to generously benefit society. Warren Buffet, one of the richest men in America, escapes the trap of excessiveness by living in the same modest home in Omaha without great displays of wealth and a jet-setting lifestyle.

Whether we are rich or poor, or somewhere in between, it behooves us to always remember the words of Jesus in Mark 8:36: "What shall it profit a man, if he shall gain the whole world and lose his own soul?"

Greed often demands a very high price...just ask King Midas.

Prayer: Dear Good and Loving Father, protect us from ourselves, and from trusting in our 401's and portfolios. Forgive us for neglecting Your Word and not putting You first in our lives. Amen.

17

Never Give Up!

Hebrews 12:1b ....let us run with perseverance the race marked out for us.

When Winston Churchill was invited to speak at Harrow School in England in 1941, he delivered words that resonated in his inimitable orator's voice throughout the auditorium.

They were words worthy of being written on parchment scrolls, tied with satin ribbons, and flung out to each new generation. He said: "Never give in— never give in— never, *never* in nothing great or small, large or petty— never give in except to convictions of honor and good sense." ("in anything" would be more grammatically correct than "in nothing"–but that's just the English teacher in me speaking)

Surely what he exhorted that day served as a torchlight to guide those young men throughout their lives, and the "never give in" (sometimes quoted as "never give up") words echo down the halls of the decades, speaking not only to school children, but to all of us.

Thomas Alva Edison once wrote, "Our greatest weakness lies in giving up. The most certain way to succeed is always to try just one more time." He must have been following his own advice when he tried so many times to develop a successful light bulb; he declared that he knew 999 ways a light bulb *didn't* work, but he wouldn't give up. Eventually he hit pay dirt and *Eureka!*...his bulb lit up!

Supposedly the cleaning product "Formula 409" was so-named because it took 408 tries before the chemists developed a successful recipe. Who knows how many other things in this world came into being because someone wouldn't give up! Indeed, many great works are wrought, not by strength or brilliance, but by perseverance. Thomas Foxwell Buxton expressed it well: "With ordinary talent and extraordinary perseverance all things are attainable."

The principles of perseverance apply also to our faith lives. Sometimes we get discouraged and the testing becomes just too much. Perhaps we are disappointed with others in the church, or we are disappointed in ourselves. Perhaps our prayers just seem to bump off the ceiling, and the sleeve of our faith is ragged and weary. The Bible encourages us to endure.

"Blessed is the man who perseveres under trial, because when he has stood the test, he will receive the crown of life that God has promised to those who love him." (James 1:12)

Perseverance has its rewards, whether temporal or eternal—or both!

Prayer: Faithful Jesus, how thankful I am that You didn't give up on us, but persevered to deliver us from our sins and give us a place in heaven with you. Keep us from giving up, and empower us to endure. Amen.

18

Warning from Lazarus

Read the story of the rich man and Lazarus in Luke 16:19-25

Luke 16:26 And besides all this, between us and you a great chasm has been fixed, so that those who want to go from here to you cannot, nor can anyone cross over from there to us.

Have you ever wondered what messages those who have died might be trying to transmit to us, the living? Would they have words of warning coming from the wisdom of the after-life which they are now experiencing?

Would they be yelling across that vast expanse that separates us with such words as the following: "Don't run around with that crowd of people!" "Don't get in that car with the tipsy driver!" "Don't marry that immature, selfish person!" "Don't neglect your children!" "Adhere to the Ten Commandments!" "Put Christ in your life...listen to his teachings, and be concerned for the needs of others!"

The dead rich man described in Luke was suffering horribly in the fiery torment of hell.

He had lived in luxury while residing on earth, coming and going his merry way with little regard for Lazarus, the sore-inflicted beggar who sat at his gate. Poor Lazarus hungered for even a few of the crumbs that fell from the rich man's table.

But the story of Lazarus has a happy ending. After his death the angels carry him to be at Abraham's side and he receives the comforts of heaven. The rich man, on the other hand, ends up in hell where he longs for even a few drops of cool water on his tongue. He calls out to Abraham, begging for Lazarus to come to his aid. When he learns there is a great gulf between heaven and hell that cannot be traversed, he then pleads for Lazarus to be allowed to go and warn his five brothers. He believes that if someone from the dead speaks to them, they will listen. But Father Abraham replies, "If they do not listen to Moses and the Prophets, they will not be convinced even if someone rises from the dead." (Luke 16:31)

Those who have gone before us cannot warn us of the eternal consequences of our choices and attitudes while we are here on earth, but the Prophets do still speak to us in the Scriptures, as in the recorded story of Lazarus in Luke 16... if we are willing to listen.

Prayer: Dear Father of Abraham and the Prophets and Lazarus and all the saints in glory, what will it take for us to hear? Unstop our ears! Open our eyes to Your Word! Fill our hearts with love and concern for others. In the name of Jesus, Amen.

19

How to Be a Ruby Wife

Read Proverbs 31

Prov. 31:10 A wife of noble character who can find? She is worth far more than rubies.

"Worth far more than rubies!" Now why did wise old Solomon use rubies in his praise of a worthy wife in Proverbs 31? In explaining her great value, would not "sheep on a hundred hills" or "many cauldrons of olive oil" been a more practical example of wealth to the Jewish people of olden days. But, no, he chose "rubies," those blood-red, magnificent stones as his gauge of extreme worth.

My Bible dictionary tells me that gems were very important to the Hebrew people. They reveled in the beauty of gemstones and used them for personal adornment and as gifts. David's crown was set with gems. Precious stones were used in seals and breastplates. Aaron's breastplate contained twelve stones representing the twelve tribes of Israel. ("Nelson's Illustrated Bible Dictionary," Thomas Nelson Publishers, 1986, pg. 569)

Thus, the Jewish people could really relate to a noble woman being compared to a gem of great value, the ruby. This woman looks well to the ways of her household, and she is always busy providing food and clothing for them. She "opens

her arms to the poor and extends her hands to the needy."
(Prov. 31:20) "She speaks with wisdom....and does not eat the
bread of idleness." (Prov. 31:26a and 27b)

The noble wife of Proverbs 31 is a hard act to follow. She
is busy night and day serving others and pursuing excellence,
even "buying fields"! She glows like a ruby. Take a stroll through
a mall and look into the windows of a jewelry store, survey the
exquisite beauty of diamonds and rubies and sigh: "Lord, I can
never be as perfect and priceless as one of these."

However, take heart, for the key to being a ruby-wife is in
the last part of Proverbs 31, verse 30: "but a woman who fears
the Lord is to be praised." If a woman truly loves God, the gifts
of His Spirit will make her beautiful in a way that Avon and Max
Factor could never attain to; her Godly inner beauty will make
her more precious than whole mountains of precious gems.

*Prayer: Dear Lord God, I stand in awe before You and
adore You. Please give me the gifts of Your Spirit so I can
be a ruby wife, mother, and citizen of the world. In the
name of Jesus I pray. Amen.*

20

Sleepwalker Alert

Romans 13:11 And do this, understanding the present time. The hour has come for you to wake up from your slumber, because our salvation is nearer now than when we first believed.

I Thess. 5:6 So then, let us not be like others, who are asleep, but let us be alert and self-controlled.

Have you heard this one? A Sunday school teacher was dismissing her class of little children to go into the sanctuary for the church service. "Now why is it important to be quiet in church?" she asked. One little girl replied, "Because the people are sleeping."

As cute as that story is, the little girl may have hit upon an element of truth. Though most eyes are open and no snoring heard (generally), there may be a modicum of truth as the thoughts of some people may be flitting elsewhere. Perhaps concern over the Sunday dinner to be prepared at home, the car needing an oil change, the apparel of those sitting around us, the distraction of children, a headache, making plans for the upcoming week, emotional turmoil– any of these and more may be a hindrance to our full participation in the worship service.

Many of us look like we're awake, but we may be faking it—slumbering on auto pilot, and then sleepwalking out the front doors and becoming immersed once again in the status quo.

On a night of great anguish— the night of His arrest leading to the crucifixion— Jesus and the disciples went to the Garden of Gethsemane on the Mount of Olives where Jesus asked them to pray that they would not fall into temptation. Jesus went a little further away and "stormed the gates of heaven"— my description of his impassioned prayer where He was ministered to by an angel and sweat great drops of blood. Jesus knew what lay ahead and the importance of prayer.

Imagine His dismay when he went back to the disciples and found them snoozing. "'Why are you sleeping?' he asked them. 'Get up and pray so that you will not fall into temptation.'" (Luke 22:46)

Surely our Lord is also dismayed when He finds us sleeping in church, or in the garden, or wherever we are in the arena of our lives. Are we Christians not sometimes sleepwalking through our days? The Apostle Paul cautions us in I Thess. 5:6 to wake up, be alert, and self- controlled. The moments are counting down towards midnight and we need to be fully awake and living in Him!

Prayer: Dear Lord Jesus, help us to come out of our sleepwalking fog, and listen earnestly to Your Word, pray devoutly, and be awake in You! Amen.

21

A Brother's Sacrifice

Proverbs 17:17 A friend is always loyal, and a brother is born to help in time of need. (NLT)

Once upon a time in fifteenth century Germany, there were two brothers who were artistically talented and wished to pursue a higher education. However, there were eighteen children in their family and they knew their father could not afford to send them to the nearby Academy in Nuremberg. So they made a pact: they would toss a coin; the winner would go to the Academy to study art and the loser would work to support him. Then after the first brother graduated, he would take his turn and support the second so he could also fulfil his dreams.

Albrecht Durer won the toss and went happily off to refine his talents, while his brother Albert took a job in the mines and sent money regularly to Albrecht. Albrecht was very successful at the Academy and his art won many accolades. Meanwhile, each day, Albert went down into the dark and dangerous mines where his hands took a terrible beating.

When Albrecht graduated, the family had a party to celebrate. Albrecht raised his glass to toast his brother who had made his education possible. "Now," he said, "it is your turn to attend the Academy and I will support you!"

IN JARS OF CLAY

Albert arose and held out his hands in which the bones in every finger had been smashed, and the right hand was arthritic. With tears running down his cheeks, he said, "There is no way that I could hold a pen and draw the fine lines which would be required. It is too late for me!"

One wonders at the loyalty and diligence of Albert. Afterall, he could have sent a message after the first smashed finger and called off the deal. Instead he labored on and by his sacrifice, he gifted the world with the exquisitely-executed art of Albrecht Durer.

Later, the accomplished brother determined to draw a pair of hands, palms together, fingers pointed upward like a steeple, and the model for his masterpiece, known as "The Praying Hands," was the work-worn hands of his brother, Albert.

A story of a brother's sacrifice is always touching. Sometimes it is life-giving. Consider the case of Jesus whose hands were smashed by spikes when He was nailed to the cross where He gave the ultimate sacrifice for His brothers. Jesus, Himself, said prior to his execution: "Greater love has no one than this, that one lay down his life for his friends." (John 15:13)

What a beautiful work of art Jesus wrought: the Salvation of the souls of millions of people!

Prayer: Dear Brother and Friend, Jesus, thank you for laying down Your life in sacrifice for our sins. Your love for us is beyond knowing... breath-taking and overwhelming! We respond in praise and devotion. Amen.

22

One Go-Around

Hebrews 9:27 And as it is appointed unto men once to die, but after this the judgment. (KJV)

Man dies once– then it's kaput, fini, THE END– no do-overs! No reincarnation into butterflies, birds, or yaks! One lifetime, however short or long, that's all we get. One chance at mortal life, and then eternity.

Nathaniel Hawthorne wrote an interesting short story entitled "Dr. Heideggar's Experiment" in which he presents the premise: what if– what if we could become young once again and have a second chance at life, would we make the same mistakes?

In Hawthorne's moralistic tale, four elderly people who had polluted their lives in the foolishness of young adulthood and succumbed to greed, vanity, debauchery and immorality are offered an elixir from the fountain of youth. Although they beg the doctor for the potion and promise that their lives will be different the second time around, one can see in their whirling trip backward through time that they are up to their old tricks again. Their "do-overs" fail as they once again succumb to their former downfalls.

There are no magic potions to ensure change in this one

"go-around" through life, and then will come the judgment. The past is the past. As much as we would like to wipe out certain words and actions, there is nothing we can do to erase even one moment that we have already lived. We cannot go back and change anything, but we can start down a different path by asking God to forgive our past sins and mistakes, and then spend the rest of this one "go round" walking with Jesus, trusting and believing in Him to make us new creations.

Just as we exist *once,* Christ died *once* "to take away the sins of many people." (Hebrews 9:28a) and by grace we are saved (See Eph. 2:8-9). Let's not waste this *one* opportunity to finish the course by living a meaningful and productive life from here on out.

Prayer: Dear Lord Jesus, thank you for the singular gift of mortal life and all the blessings You bestow on us during our journey here on earth. Help us not to waste our days, but to live them well and for your glory! Amen.

23

Our Best Friend

John 15:15 I no longer call you servants, because a servant does not know his master's business. Instead, I have called you friends, for everything that I learned from my Father I have made known to you.

Friends weave themselves like gleaming threads of many colors in and out of the tapestry of our lives. Some threads endure while others drop from the pattern. It's just a fact of life that some friendships don't last forever– time and circumstances change relationships. However, I was a little taken aback recently when I read of a study that found that "most of us change half our good buddies every seven years." ("Family Circle" Magazine, 11-1-11, pg. 73)

Certainly, friends do become separated by distance, changing interest, boredom, or sadly, by "falling-outs." The loss of a friend is often traumatic. When our son was seven years old, his best pal and playmate, whose father was a pastor, moved miles away to a different parish. I still remember that as I tucked my son into bed that first night, his voice quivered and his eyes watered as he asked, "Will I ever see John again?"

Since that time, he's learned the indelible truth that friends will come, and friends will go, but one *true* friend is always near, and that friend is Jesus. He is as close as our hearts. He always cares, and we can always trust and confide in Him.

"What A Friend We Have In Jesus" is the beloved hymn whose words were composed by Joseph Scriven. When Joseph's fiancee died on the eve of their wedding, he found comfort in his dearest friend, Jesus. Later, when Joseph's mother became ill, he comforted her with words he had penned: "What a Friend we have in Jesus, all our sins and griefs to bear! What a privilege to carry everything to God in prayer!" He concluded: "Do thy friends despise, forsake thee? Take it to the Lord in prayer; in his arms He'll take and shield thee– Thou wilt find a solace there."

Ah, yes, earthly friends come and go, blessings sent our way. For seven years, or seventy, they grace our lives. But no friend will ever be as enduring, dependable, or as wonderful as Jesus!

Prayer: Dear Jesus, thank you for calling us your "friends," and inviting us to keep our friendship strong with You through prayer. May I not neglect You, my dearest friend. Amen.

24

The Beauty in Ordinary Days

Ps. 16:llb In thy presence is fullness of joy, at thy right hand are pleasures forever more. (KJV)

Life happens so fast; it rushes around and through us in great flooding tides. We barely have time to stop, breathe deeply, and savor the moment. We are unable to truly appreciate each other, and the abundance of blessings we have in ordinary days.

Emily who had died in childbirth in Thornton Wilder's drama, "Our Town," is given permission by the Stage Manager to return for one day to her life in Grover's Corners, New Hampshire, around the turn of the 20th century. She chooses her twelfth birthday but finds that people are so busy and self-absorbed that they don't even really look at each other. She misses such simple and yet precious things as new-ironed dresses, sunflowers, clocks ticking, sleeping and waking up. Poignantly, she asks the Stage Manager, "Do any human beings ever realize life while they live it– every, every minute?" He replies, "No, the saints and poets, maybe they do some." Saddened by the reality that most people sleepwalk through life, she cuts short her day on earth and asks to go back to the grave.

I wonder, would we Christians be numbered among those saints who are conscious of the absolute wonder of existence?

Are we present in every moment, recognizing the fullness of joy that is ours as we walk with our Lord? Are we overwhelmed with the beauty of the sun winking through the blushing orange and yellow leaves of a maple tree? Do we relish the essence of fresh laundered sheets, apples bubbling on the stove, the calm at dusk, the sound of our loved ones' voices? Do we praise the Lord for all the taken-for-granted blessings of ordinary days?

Surely the third act of "Our Town" is not so much about an after-life as it is about life– the wonder of life– and how blind we are as we travel through it.

Prayer: Fairest Lord Jesus, when I am in Your presence, things can be so immediate and so pungently beautiful. Your Spirit lends more brightness to every moment of the day, and encourages me to count my blessings in ordinary things. And I also praise You for the extraordinary joy of knowing You as my Savior. Amen.

25

Building Spiritual Muscle

Ps. 103:2 Praise the Lord, O my soul, and forget not all his benefits.

Ps. 78:11 They forgot what he had done, the wonders he had shown them.

"Use it or lost it," was a mantra often used by the physical fitness guru, Jack LaLanne. For years he demonstrated on television a plethora of gyrations to tone and stretch every perceivable muscle of the body and he, himself, was an example of a very healthy and toned physique. He knew the importance of daily exercise and he never forgot to employ it.

"Use it or lose it" also applies to the mind. As people grow older, brain matter, just like abs and quads, may also atrophy. We are encouraged to stimulate our brains by reading, writing, learning new skills and/or languages, playing games such as Scrabble, and working crossword puzzles. Like the muscles of the body, the mind needs to be challenged and stretched daily.

It would only follow that "Use it or lose it" could also apply to the spirit which also may atrophy if not stimulated regularly. In prayer and Bible study we stretch our faith and give it strength and resilience. In worship and praise we center ourselves in the presence of God and are open to spiritual refilling. If we neglect these things and forget our Lord and all his benefits, we are in danger of a shrinking faith.

The Israelites seemed to have a short attention span and were troubled with memory loss. Psalm 78 recounts the many ways the Lord had helped them– delivering them from bondage, parting the sea for their escape, leading them in the wilderness, feeding them manna and providing water. All the miracles and wonders He showed them are recounted in the 72 verses of Psalm 78. And though they rebelled against Him or ignored Him, the Lord had such patience with them and did not forget them. We would do well not to test Him as they did.

How wonderful to have spiritual muscle to resist the temptations of the world, and to live in Him. If we forget the Lord, and ignore spiritual training, are we not putting our souls in jeopardy?

Prayer: Our Father, do not forget us and help us not to forget You. Help us exercise the spiritual muscle that You have placed in every soul. Make our faith strong and healthy in You. Amen.

26

The Indestructible Word

John 1:1 In the beginning was the Word, and the Word was with God, and the Word was God.

In many lands throughout many eras of history, the Bible has been banned. There have been tyrants, despots, and enemies who have tried to eradicate the Word of God from the earth.

In Communist countries during the Cold War, Scriptures were confiscated and thrown into huge bonfires. Those people who managed to possess Scriptures were living in great danger.

Brother Andrew was a young Dutch man who dared to smuggle Bibles into countries behind the Iron Curtain during the late 1950's. In his classic book, "God's Smuggler," he recounts how he trusted the Lord to help him deliver Bibles. In one notable experience as he began entry into Romania, cars were stopped and searched at a checkpoint. He waited in line and watched the guards literally tear cars apart, removing hub caps and seats, searching through engines. Praying for God's help, he was led to take the Bibles and place them in plain sight right beside him on the front seat. In an amazing happenstance the guards waved him through and then proceeded to dismantle the car behind him. Once again Brother Andrew had witnessed a miracle of God's provision and protection.

The Word has been here from the beginning (John 1:1) and we can be sure it will be here until the end. Though silenced in certain times and places, it continues to rise up like an indestructible yeast in the affairs of history.

Even though there are those who would ban it; those who would burn it; those who would stamp it out, the Word of God endures. As it is written in Ps. 119:89: "Your word, O Lord, is eternal; it stands firm in the heavens." It will never be quenched!

Prayer: In the beginning was You, Lord, Author of the Bible; how we love Your precious Word. Thank you for those who have translated it and carried it to far lands, and for those who have implanted it into our own hearts. We praise You for Your Holy, indestructible Word! Amen.

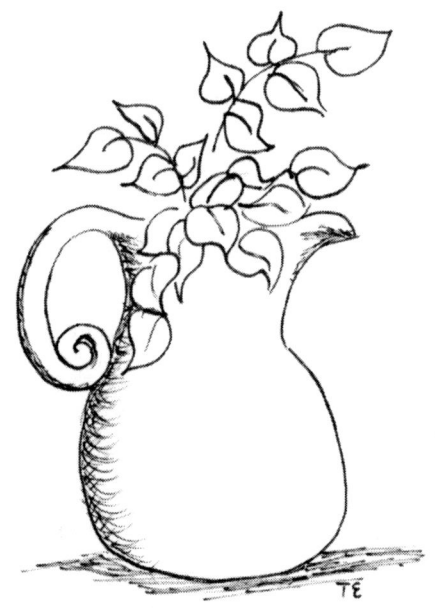

27

Burst into a Song

Luke 1: 46-55 Mary's Song (The Magnificat)

Luke 1: 46-49 And Mary said: "My soul praises the Lord and my spirit rejoices in God my Savior, for he has been mindful of the humble state of his servant. From now on all generations will call me blessed, for the Mighty One has done great things for me— holy is his name.

"I Whistle a Happy Tune" is a song from Rodger's and Hammerstein's Broadway musical, "The King and I." Anna, who has traveled to the country of Siam to teach the children of the king, reveals how she faces her fears when she lyrically proclaims, "Whenever I feel afraid I hold my head erect and whistle a happy tune so no one will suspect I'm afraid."

Could that have been the situation when Mary of Nazareth, over two thousand years ago, was approached by the angel Gabriel and told that she was going to bear a child with God as its father? She surely could have had a bundle of doubts and fears about this whole unorthodox situation, and might have sung Anna's song. Instead, she burst into her beautiful Magnificat that was not a disguise of her fears, but an affirmation of her faith. Upon hearing the proclamation by Gabriel, one couldn't blame her if she had been besieged by doubts. There was the possibility that Joseph would break their engagement when he heard the unbelievable news. And, how would her parents react, and their friends and neighbors? She would surely be the hot topic of conversation at the town well!

Her reputation was at stake. Her family and groom-to-be might disown her, and put her away quietly. How would she manage on her own? Her whole pregnancy could have been fraught with questions, fears, and doubts. Even at the end of her term it must have been very scary for this teenage girl to deliver her first-born child in a smelly stable without even a mid-wife near!

But young Mary seemed to accept the situation with such calm aplomb– *faith*– and because of that faith she was able to burst forth into a song when she visited her cousin Elizabeth early on to tell her the news. Mary's gladness resounds like bells down through the generations in the Magnificat. No wonder the Lord chose her as the bearer of His Son whom He was sending into the world to be a Savior for mankind. He already knew that she would be totally willing to submit to His will, and would be faithful through it all. So when we are facing perplexing problems, or seemingly impossible situations, we would do well to follow Mary's example, and burst into a song! When challenges beset us and doubts assail us, we have the same God of Mary at our side, and with her we can "magnify" our Lord and place our trust fully in Him.

Yes, we can hum a happy tune, not to cover up our fears as in the "King and I" song, but to *actually* be unafraid as we believe in a loving, all-powerful God, and praise Him with all our hearts, just as Mary did.

Prayer: Our Father in heaven, help us submit to Your will and trust You fully in all things. In all the universe there is none more glorious than You; Your marvelous deeds proceed us throughout the generations, and we praise You! Amen.

28

A Lost Boy and a Lost Sheep

The Parable of the Lost Sheep

Matthew 18:10-14 "See that you do not look down on one of these little ones. For I tell you that their angels in heaven always see the face of my Father in heaven.

"What do you think? If a man owns a hundred sheep, and one of them wanders away, will he not leave the ninety-nine on the hills and go to look for the one that wandered off. In the same way your Father in heaven is not willing that any of these little ones should be lost.

What are some predicaments that can cause a sheep to be separated and lost from his shepherd? Perhaps the curly-haired little animal could wander off and get caught in some brambles. Perhaps he could slip into a ravine, or be attacked by wolves. In the story that Jesus tells in Matthew 18, the shepherd is so distraught over one missing little lamb that he will leave the flock and go looking all over for it. He still has ninety-nine sheep, but even one little lamb who has gone astray is worth the search, and the trouble of carrying it back to the fold.

One day I was shopping downtown and I lost our two-year-old son. One moment he was standing beside me in Woolworth's and the next moment he was gone. I had stopped to examine some merchandise, and let go of his hand for only a few breaths of time, but that is all it took for him to disappear from my sight. I looked up and down a few aisles before I asked a clerk for help. She enlisted another clerk and we searched the whole store— no little Reed. By this time I was getting rather frantic. I went out into the street where a multitude of dangers could have swallowed up my child. I went up and down the main street, my eyes pleading to see a little blond boy in a red shirt and navy overalls. But he was nowhere to be seen. My heart dropped into my shoe tops— such a horrible feeling to lose a child! I got into the car without Reed in his car seat where he was on the trip uptown... where he should be now! I drove seven blocks home and called my husband who worked across town. "What shall I do?" I cried into the telephone. "Call the police... meanwhile I'll go downtown and look myself," he advised.

About ten minutes later, my husband called me back. "Reed has been found...a man brought him to me here at the shop." The man saw a little boy wandering alone down the street (nearly three blocks from Woolworth's and through two stop lights, which he had no idea how to navigate!) The man had never seen Reed before in his life, but he saw a resemblance to my husband, which is uncanny because first of all Reed's hair was whitish-blond and my husband's was dark brown. Reed's eyes were green, my husband's were brown! Nonetheless, I thanked God profusely for what seemed like nothing less than a miracle, and for the fact that my wandering child had been delivered safely back into the fold with me!

A lost lamb....a lost boy....a lost soul! How the shepherd felt, how I felt...that's how God feels about every one of his children. He doesn't want to lose even one believer! How much He cares for each of us! When we go astray, he is the "hound of heaven," pursuing us; the "good shepherd" longing to once again gather us to His bosom.

Prayer: Oh, Good and Wonderful Lord, thank You that by Your providence You brought my lost son back to me. The feeling of loss that I had that day helps me to realize how very much You love us— with an everlasting love that bids us to take Your hand and stay safely by Your side. Amen.

29

Of Fleas and Sharks

I Thessalonians 5:18 ....give thanks in all circumstances for this is God's will for you in Christ Jesus.

Corrie and Betsie ten Boom had just entered the horrors of Ravensbruck, a German concentration camp in World War II. The middle-aged women had been hiding Jews in a secret room in their Dutch home until an informer caused them to be arrested by the Gestapo.

Corrie had been able to successfully smuggle a Bible into the camp, a miracle of God's provision. Now Betsie wanted them to join in a prayer of thanksgiving, not only for the Bible which would end up providing hope and sustenance for so many women, but for all the circumstances they now encountered, which included even the fleas in their barracks.

Corrie joined in giving thanks for the packed and suffocating crowds, all jammed together in this smelly place, but fleas were too much! "Betsie," she said, "there's no way even God can make me grateful for a flea."

"Give thanks in *all* circumstances," Betsie quoted the verse in Thessalonians; "It doesn't say 'in pleasant circumstances.' Fleas are a part of this place where God has put us."

And so dutifully Corrie thanked God for the biting, annoy-some fleas which in future days did prove to be a blessing. The center room of the barracks where the sisters had their bunks was so heavily infected with fleas that the guards would not come near them, and every night Corrie and Betsie were able to minister with their Bible to all those hurting souls in the light of one dim bulb. ("The Hiding Place" by Corrie ten Boom with John and Elizabeth Sherrill, Chosen Books, 1971.)

In another case from those war years, a curse actually became a blessing when survivors of a Naval battle were afloat in the Philippine Sea after their ship (the USS Samuel B. Roberts Destroyer Escort) was riddled by shells from Japanese ships in the Battle of Samar Island. Stinking oil from their damaged vessel had fouled the water and in turn, coated their faces and hair, and stung their eyes. The battle had been ordeal enough, but now the American sailors struggled to survive in the sea with their bodies coated in oil. Oil which turned out to be a blessing–sharks were adverse to it and didn't come near them. The oil also turned out to be an effective sunscreen, important since they were afloat several days before they were finally rescued! ("The Last of the Tin Can Sailors" by James D. Hornfischer, Bantam-Dell, 2004)

How often in God's great design do such things happen.... when even fleas and oil- drenched seas can be a boon! How compelling that each of us can thank God for unlikely future blessings in all the circumstances of our lives, and how wonderful to stand back and watch His grace "work everything together for good for those who love Him, for those who are called according to His purpose." (Romans 8:28)

Prayer: Thank you, dear good and gracious Father, that You always hover near us in all the situations of our lives, anxious to amaze us with Your loving care. We praise You in all things. Amen.

30

Are You Salty?

Matt. 5:13 You are the salt of the earth; but if the salt has become tasteless, how can it be made salty again? It is no longer good for anything, except to be thrown out and trampled under foot by men. (NASB)

Open any cupboard door in America these days and you will surely find a round cardboard container of table salt! This staple of our kitchens was once a rare and coveted substance. In Bible times when there was no refrigeration, the people relied heavily on salt to preserve their food and guard their health. Salt was not just an *extra,* it was a *necessity*! Thus, the camel trains bearing salt were probably a very welcome sight.

In fact, salt was an important trade item. Some workers, including Roman soldiers, even received part of their salary in salt. (Perhaps that's where we get the expression, "He's worth his salt"!)

Besides preservation, salt enhanced the flavor of tasteless foods. Job 6:6 reflected on this important aspect of salt when the question was asked, "Is tasteless food eaten without salt?" (In those days, the effect of salt on blood pressure was probably unknown, so they would have suffered no qualms about being generous with the use of it.)

Although we in this century may be cautious about the amount of salt we ingest, we recognize the value of salt as a healing agent on the outside of our bodies. A wound subjected to ocean water may sting for a while, but soon the healing effect can be evidenced. Salt is used in the treatment of certain skin conditions such as psoriasis, and in saline bandages to guard wounds against infection and promote healing. Salt is very useful in easing allergies and keeping sinuses healthy. My husband will attest that daily rinsing with a saline solution really does cut down on sinus infections!

Thus, we note three great uses for salt– in food preservation, as a flavor-enhancer, and as a healing agent! It is no wonder that Jesus chose saltiness as an analogy for good discipleship.

If we are Christlike we will "flavor" the world around us with the savory taste of goodness, righteousness and peace. And if we spread the Gospel message, we will be dispensers of the great "preservative" of men's souls.

The philosopher Henry David Thoreau said, "The mass of men lead lives of quiet desperation," but we believe that there is an antidote to this desperation in the hope and "healing" of God's Word. We carry this precious element with us to shake upon the hurting people of the earth.

As Christians, we dare not lose our saltiness, for we will become useless to the Kingdom.

Prayer: Dearest Jesus, help us by the Holy Spirit to be agents of kindness, love, and healing. Make us effective and "salty" disciples for You! Amen.

31

Bullet-Proof

Read Eph. 6:10-18 The Armor of God

Eph. 6:16&17 In addition to all this, take up the shield of faith, with which you can extinguish all the flaming arrows of the evil one.

The Word of God has great protective powers in ways one wouldn't ordinarily contemplate. There have been occasions reported where a Bible carried in the vest pocket of a soldier's uniform has actually stopped a bullet and saved his life. During the Civil War many soldiers wore their Testaments into battle.

For instance, one young man from Massachusetts signed up to fight for the Union. Before he left home his sister presented him with a pocket-sized Bible which he carried over his heart. During the battle of Shiloh, a bullet crashed against his body, but was stopped in its flight by the pages of the Holy Book. His only complication was a bruised chest from the impact of the ball. (From an article, "Bible Stops Bullet, Saves Soldier's Life," published in "The National Preacher and Village Pulpit," an 1861 periodical.)

Another instance of "Bible armor" was a Testament carried by Walter G. Jones in his "blouse" pocket. This time, the Bible the soldier carried protected him not only once, but twice in two separate skirmishes. An upper corner of the book reveals a ragged hole which it sustained in the battle of Cedar Creek, VA, Oct. 19, 1864. The second hole was the result of a bullet which pierced the Testament in the battle of Appomattox in 1865. Fascinating pictures of these Bibles and others can be viewed at www.old-picture.com/civil-war/Bullet-Bible-with-Hole. htm.

"The Devil and Tom Walker," an early American tale written by Washington Irving, rather humorously portrays a man who makes a deal with the devil. The greedy Tom Walker trades his soul for wealth, but as the day of reckoning closes in, Tom starts carrying a Bible around as one would hold on to an amulet, or lucky charm. Instead of a Bible in *front* of his heart, he should have put the Holy Word *into* his heart, for the devil carries Tom off, clad in his nightshirt one evening, without his Bible near.

With both the soldiers and Tom Walker, it was what was *inside* that little black book which was necessary for the soul's salvation and protection for eternity. Physical life may be spared for a few more years as in the stories above, but eventually it is the *content* of the Good Book which protects our souls.

We need the Bible, not as an under-read epistle gathering dust on the coffee table, but as an inspired vehicle through which the Holy Spirit works to generate faith and save our eternal lives. The Word of God is our shield, our full-metal armor, our eternal protection.

Prayer: Our Lord God, we are so vulnerable and unsafe as we live out our days on earth! Help us to constantly put on the strong armor of Your Word to protect us on our march toward eternity. Amen.

32

The Legacy of Ruth

Ruth 1:16&17 And Ruth said, Intreat me not to leave thee, or to return from following after thee: for whether thou goest I will go; and where thou lodgest, I will lodge: thy people shall be my people, and thy God my God:

Where thou diest, will I die, and there will I be buried: the Lord do so to me and more also, if ought but death part thee and me. (KJV)

The relationship between a mother-in-law and a daughter-in-law is often tenuous, so one perhaps wonders at the devotion of Ruth to her husband's mother, Naomi.

After the death of her husband and her two sons, Naomi was bidding her two Moabite daughters-in-law "goodbye" as she intended to return to her homeland of Judah. Naomi and her husband and two sons had relocated years ago to the land of Moab because of a famine. Now her husband and sons were dead and she wanted to go home to Judah again.

While in Moab, her two sons had come of age and had married Moabite women, Ruth and Orpah. Naomi told the two women that she had nothing to offer them and advised them to stay among their people in Moab.

Orpah agreed, packed her things and went back to her family, but Ruth declined. "No, I'm going with you, and even though I am a Gentile, I want to dwell among your people, and worship your God!" (My paraphrase of the much more beautiful declaration of faithfulness in Ruth 1:16)

Naomi must have had some apprehension about this. She knew how much the Israelites hated the Moabites and she realized that Ruth might not be well-received in Bethlehem. Also, she had no men to offer for protection and provision. As for jobs, no Moabites need apply.

But Ruth would not be denied. Her love for, and loyalty to her mother-in-law compelled her to go as a stranger into a foreign land with no prospects once they got there. Naomi gave in and they began what might have been a hot and arduous journey as they traveled the Moab back country, crossed the Jordan River, and finally made their way to Bethlehem.

One wonders if Naomi was a very good companion, for in her own words she said that she was a "bitter" woman. (See Ruth 1:20) But Ruth lovingly cared for her, and upon arriving in Judah she went out to do the back-breaking work of gleaning barley that was left behind in the fields so they would have something to eat. Probably Ruth was scorned by the other women who also gleaned in the fields. Maybe the catcalls made her homesick for her own people. A lesser woman than Ruth might have taken the next bus headed east out of Bethlehem.

But Ruth endured and in a turn of events, married Boaz, a kinsman of Naomi's, and to their union was born Obed, the grandfather of King David who was in the lineage of Jesus Christ, the Messiah.

Ruth's loyalty to Naomi and her hunger to know Naomi's God were rewarded in a very big way, for she was a link in the chain of God's great plan for the Salvation of His people, Israelites and Gentiles alike!

Aren't we glad that Ruth didn't catch a bus headed east out of Bethlehem!

Prayer: Dear Father of the Nations, Ruth lived out her pledge of love to Naomi, and we would ask You to also give us generous and willing hearts so that we may live out our calling in You with love and loyalty! In Jesus we pray, Amen.

33

Dwell on Lovely Things

Philippians 4:8 Finally, brothers, whatever is true, whatever is noble, whatever is right, whatever is pure, whatever is lovely, whatever is admirable— if anything is excellent or praiseworthy— think about such things.

William Wordsworth was wandering about the English countryside one day when he chanced upon a breath-taking sight— hundreds of golden daffodils, "fluttering and dancing" in the breeze "along the margin of a bay." He stood gazing, drinking in the glorious sight, little thinking how it would benefit him in the days to come. Reflecting on it later, he wrote, "For oft when on my couch I lie— In vacant or in pensive mood, they flash upon the inward eye which is the bliss of solitude— And then my heart with pleasure fills, And dances with the daffodils." (From "The Daffodils" by William Wordsworth)

Just as Wordsworth's mood was lifted by recalling a lovely image, conversely our minds can be weighed down by many of the gloomy images that often come our way. I know people who deliberately avoid watching the newscasts on television or looking at newspapers because there are so many negative images which produce sadness and depression. Focusing on the evil in the world as well as the problems in our personal lives can overwhelm us, and if we aren't careful, our "couches" may become watered with our tears as we lie in "pensive" moods.

Our thought processes are strongly related to our outlook on life! We often have to train the brain to focus on the positives of life instead of becoming laden with the negatives. Just as Wordsworth had a field of daffodils to brighten his day, surely we also have lovely sights filed away on the "photos.com" of our memory. Sunset on a lake, moist pine needles on a fragrant forest floor, a child chasing butterflies in a field of purple clover...hopefully, we have those "daffodil" moments upon which to dwell, images to calm our souls and lift us up.

It is also important to have Bible verses tucked away among our mind treasures, golden Words to calm our souls with powerful and hope-filled messages from God. Lovely words like the message from Philippians which is quoted above. The verse following that passage concludes: "And the God of peace will be with you." (Phil. 4:9b)

Peace will come if we lie upon our couches and think on things that are noble, right, pure, praiseworthy and admirable. We will be uplifted and happier if we concentrate on the myriads of blessings which dance around us like millions of golden daffodils.

Prayer: Dear Lord God, You fashioned our marvelous brains and You instruct us in ways to keep them well-tuned. Help us to repel negative thoughts and to dwell on ones that are positive and pleasing to You! Amen.

34

The Grapes of Glory

John 15:1 (Jesus said) "I am the true vine, and My Father is the vinedresser. Every branch in me that does not bear fruit, He takes away; and every branch that bears fruit, He prunes it so that it may bear more fruit." (NASB)

John 15: 7&8 "If you abide in Me and My words abide in you, ask whatever you wish, and it will be done for you. My Father is glorified by this, that you bear much fruit, and so prove to be My disciples." (NASB)

When I was a child we moved to a farm where the previous owner had planted an extensive orchard and a grape arbor. We enjoyed the fruits of that farmer's labors— especially the arbor in September when the globes of deep purple Concord grapes hung heavy on the vines and reached their tantalizing peak of flavor. The lush, earthy smell of ripened grapes infused the air of the arbor beckoning us, as well as assorted flying insects. We loved to pluck the marbles of fruit and chew on the sweet, juicy skins, often spitting out the gelatinous centers encasing the seeds.

However, after a few years, the vines died out and our grape arbor summers came to an end. Perhaps my parents weren't adept as vinedressers or had more pressing things on their minds.

Maybe a lack of pruning was the culprit. Of late, I have learned that one must not be timid about pruning grapes— aggressive pruning makes the vine hardier and stronger. Excess vegetation shades the grapes from the nourishment of the sun and steals the sap. Too much shade produces fewer grapes and ones of less desirable quality. Also, low growing canes should be removed from the trunk in the pruning for they may touch the ground and become diseased in wet conditions. In time, the disease will spread and kill out the arbor. Vines need to be trained to a wire or trellis which keeps them off the ground to discourage infections and to support the fruit as it ripens.

Jesus used the beautiful analogy of a grape vine when he said in the 15th chapter of John that He is the vine and we are the branches (canes). God is the vinedresser (farmer) and He prunes us so we will bear much fruit. He trims away those passions and inclinations that would deaden our spirits to God. He will protect us from overgrowth which shadows our souls and prevents the full maturing of our fruit. He will lop off those low-lying canes which would infect our souls with worldliness and the disease of sin.

God faithfully tends those who grow in the garden of faith, nourished by the sunshine and rain of His love. Jesus tells us to abide in Him and we will grow strong in Him and become healthy, productive disciples, even given whatever we ask in His name. All we have to do is *abide* in Him, live...*dwell* in Him and He and His Father will make it happen. By their Holy Spirit we cannot but help to bear fruit. Thus, we will cause Our Father, the vinedresser, to be very happy, and all we produce will glorify Him.

Prayer: Our Father, help us to abide in Jesus, attached to the vine, nourished by Your Word and Spirit so that we will bear much fine fruit for You. In His name, Amen.

35

Recognizing the Savior

John 1: 10&11 He came into the very world he created, but the world didn't recognize him. He came to his own people, and even they rejected him. (NLT)

What if I had been alive in a small town near Galilee when Jesus strode by with his twelve disciples in tow, their rough-hewn garments swirling about their ankles, their sandals crunching on the gravel pathways– even if I had all-but-rubbed elbows with this man Jesus and his "fishers of men," would I have wondered about their earnest mission and who they were? Perhaps I would have simply given them a wide berth, especially if the smell of the fishing boats still clung to them and infused the air. Would I have been remotely interested in their message, or would I have just walked on by?

And if I had heard the eager chatter of the crowds who were returning from spending an afternoon on a hill near the Sea of Galilee, would I have "tuned out" their enthusiasm? Is there a chance that I would have asked to hear more about a man who had performed healing miracles, and who had provided them a picnic from seven loaves and a few small fishes? Or would I have "shook my head" at hearing these incredulous stories and walked on?

If I had been among the women who drew water from Jacob's well in Samaria, and I had seen the man Jesus, dusty, sweaty, and tired from his journey resting there at the well, would I have been affronted when I saw him ask a Samaritan woman for a drink? Possibly, I would have been shocked that he was even speaking to a lowly Samaritan, and to a woman with a dubious reputation, at that! Would I have picked up my jug and hurried on by?

And, later, if I had been walking through Jerusalem on that alarming day and happened to see the Galilean struggling under his heavy cross as he made his way to a crucifixion, would I have washed my hands of any involvement, and hurried on by?

But in this age, I have no excuse for being clueless for I have been given the wondrous knowledge of Jesus, and how He died for me! How grateful I am that I don't need to wonder how I would have reacted in those days when He walked among his people, and whether I would have recognized Him, or whether I would be among those who rejected Him. By heaven's grace, I have the assurance of the Bible, and I *know* who He is! Therefore, I am compelled to STOP, listen to His words, and adore Him!

Prayer: Dear Jesus, my Lord and Savior, guide my steps this day so that I am attuned to You, seeking to know You better. Don't let me walk on by, but linger, to praise and honor You! Amen.

36

A Time to Sew

Eccles. 3:1,7 To everything there is a season, and a time for every purpose under the heaven... a time to rend, and a time to sew. (KJV)

Eccles. 3:12&13 I know that there is nothing better for men than to be happy and do good while they live. That way man may eat and drink and find satisfaction in all his toil– this is a gift of God.

Happiness is a treadle sewing machine! Recently the Orphan Grain Train, a Christian relief agency, shipped containers full of blankets, clothes, shoes, and other essentials for human care to orphanages in Eastern Europe and Haiti. Packed in boxes were some refurbished, old- fashioned treadle sewing machines which were bound to be unpacked with squeals of delight.

The teen girls in the orphanages will be taught to sew, and thereby, they will be able to make a living by constructing and altering clothing.

There is an old Chinese proverb that states: "Give a man a fish and you will feed him for a day, teach him to fish and you will feed him for a lifetime." Surely the same can be said for sewing. Not only can one earn a living sewing, but one can contribute to the needs of others.

Our church Missionary Circle likes to sew tops for quilts which are tied at our meetings, and then hemmed to send to foreign lands and victims struck by disasters in our own country. Often a quilt is a person's most prized possession. It provides warmth and comfort in hospitals, orphanages, or for those who lie down on dirt floors. Some tribes in Africa even use the quilts as tent awnings to protect them from the sun.

Besides all these fundamental uses of the craft of sewing, it is also a good and creative mode of self-expression, a hobby, and a way to relax. I know that sewing has afforded me many hours of worthwhile activity, and I'm never bored or lonely if my machine is threaded and some fabric awaits on my dining room table.

When my sewing machine and I are humming away, it is good to know that across the sea there are other ladies treadling away on their machines. Collectively, we know the satisfaction and blessing of sewing. As Solomon remarked in Eccles. 3, to find satisfaction in our toil is a gift of God, and we thank Him for this "time to sew."

Prayer: Dear Good and Gracious Father in Heaven, please continue to bless and empower agencies like World Relief and the Orphan Grain Train which do so much to relieve human suffering all over the world. Thank you for our sewing machines and the satisfying pursuit of sewing. Bless the work of our hands. In the name of Jesus, Amen.

37

Jesus Enchants the Little Children

Luke 18:15-17 People were also bringing babies to Jesus to have him touch them. When the disciples saw this, they rebuked them. But Jesus called the children to him and said, "Let the little children come to me, and do not hinder them, for the kingdom of God belongs to such as these. I tell you the truth, anyone who will not receive the kingdom of God like a little child will never enter it."

Children are drawn like flies to honey by warm and smiling adults. Although some artists would portray Jesus as a very somber and solemn person, this notion is dispelled by the fact that children were magnetized by the love and good humor that emanated from the man. They ran into His arms and sat upon His lap. There was nothing "off-putting" about Him. Wouldn't it have been wonderful to have been there and seen Him as He threw back His head in laughter at the sayings of these little ones! Wouldn't it have been wonderful to see how much He loved them, innocent and dewy fresh, so accepting of Him!

There are many good artists who have portrayed Jesus interacting with children but one of my favorites was rendered by David Bowman and is simply entitled "Adoration." (It may be viewed at www.lordsart.com.) In this gorgeous painting Jesus holds a little girl about four or five years old in His arms. She reclines her head against His chest, looking up into His face with absolute love and adoration. As He cups her head in his hand, Jesus looks down upon her with His eyes crinkling in laughter, and it's as if they had just shared an amusing bit of repartee. On a background palette of sunset lavenders with peach halos surrounding their heads, the artist masterfully captures the expressions of overflowing joy and love that pass between them in a transcendent moment made tangible in this lovely work of art.

Nicodemus was a learned adult who came to Jesus after night and had a hard time understanding the concept of being born again (John 3:1-21). With all his worldly wisdom and education, he failed to grasp spiritual truths with childlike faith. We must come to Jesus with unwavering dependency on His grace and mercy; we must run into His arms with the complete abandon of a child, adoring and appreciating Him like the little girl in David Bowman's painting.

If we receive Him in the manner of a child, trusting and believing in Him, we will thus be able to enter the kingdom of God. (Matt. 18:17)

Prayer: "Give me childlike faith in You, dear Lord, I need you more than anything else." (From the book, "Into His Presence" by Charles F. Stanley)

38

He Took a Stand against Evil

Ps. 116:15 Precious in the sight of the Lord is the death of His saints.

Romans 14:7&8 For none of us lives to himself, and no one dies to himself. For if we live, we live to the Lord; and if we die, we die to the Lord. Therefore, whether we live or die, we are the Lord's. (NKJV)

What rare courage does it take to become a martyr for one's beliefs?

Dietrich Bonhoeffer, a Lutheran pastor and theologian in Germany during the years of the Third Reich, could have escaped his fate. In 1939, while prospects of war were simmering, he had made a lecture tour in America. He was urged by friends to remain here because his Christian activities, including conducting an "underground seminary," were endangering his safety. But his conscience led him back to his homeland to take a stand for his convictions. A stand which ultimately cost him his life.

Perhaps he could have bypassed becoming a double-agent, but after being confronted by a leader of the Resistance and presented a folio showing some of the atrocities being performed against the Jews and others by the Gestapo, he joined the underground. He struggled with faith issues such as is it worse to "do evil" or "be evil." The Resistance wanted to "take out" Hitler, and that involved murder. All these things he had to wrestle with, as well as personal issues; he was engaged to be married to a young woman named Maria and he didn't want to endanger her with his activities.

Eventually, he was arrested and imprisoned for two years as a traitor to Germany. He conducted worship services for the other prisoners and guards during his internment, and spread a message of peace through God. In the last days of the European war he was led to his death by hanging. The camp doctor was impressed by the way he died in a way "so entirely submissive to the will of God."

Three weeks later, Hitler took his own life, and the war was soon over.

What compelled the man, Dietrich Bonhoeffer, to willingly return to his beleaguered country in 1939? And upon returning, what compelled him to engage in such a dangerous activity as double-agentry?

Only the Holy Spirit moving in his heart and soul could explain it! Only the Spirit of God living in him could have moved him to surrender all– in life– and in death!

A death which was actually only the beginning of eternal life and peace in heaven.

Prayer: Dear Lord of Truth and Righteousness, we praise You that even through the midst of darkest evil, Your Holy Spirit shines in people like Dietrich Bonhoeffer! May we, also, if in much smaller ways, live and die unto You! Amen.

Note: Some of the information for this meditation

and the partial quote by the camp doctor were taken from "Foxe: Voices of the Martyrs," Bridge-Logos, 2007. Other information came from a documentary film by Martin Doblmeier of Journey Films entitled: "Bonhoeffer: Agent of Grace" which aired previously on PBS, and is available in many film libraries.

39

The Secret of Happiness

Col 3:15b &16 ....And be thankful. Let the word of Christ dwell in your richly.

Count your blessings– name them one by one. It turns out that an "attitude of gratitude" really is the key to contentment and happiness.

As a teacher, I found it much more pleasant to work with the sunny, appreciative students than with the students who whined and complained. Kids who are grateful are "happier and more satisfied with their lives" said Jeffrey Froh, an assistant professor of psychology at Hofstra University. "They report better relationships with friends and family, higher GPA's, less envy and less depression, along with a desire to connect to their community and to give back." (As reported by Carolyn Butler in the "Washington Post," Nov. 2011.)

It has been proven that thankfulness has many healthy benefits, not only for children but for adults. Indeed, the 23rd Psalm could be paraphrased, "The Lord is my shepherd, I will not whine." The Lord has given us so much, and it is good for us to thank Him daily for His benefits, maybe even hourly, for a more heaping dose of happiness.

The story is told of a man who was besieged by robbers.

After beating him to the ground, they ran off with his wallet. When questioned, the victim, instead of bemoaning his fate, rejoiced in how fortunate he was for three different reasons. One– this was the first time he had ever been robbed– it had never happened before so that was a good thing. Two– though he had been injured, he said, "I will heal and happily I am still alive!" Three– though the wallet contained all the money he had, it wasn't much, so he really didn't lose much! Certainly, he was a "cup-half-full" kind of guy as opposed to the negative "cup-half-empty" sort.

St. Paul admonished in I Thess. 5:18 "....give thanks in all circumstances, for this is God's will for you in Christ Jesus." Sometimes we have to be creative in searching out the positives in our situations instead of dwelling on the negatives. Even when blessings are clearly remarkable, we may neglect to whole-heartedly thank God. Ten men who were plagued with the dreaded disease of leprosy called out to Jesus one day as He traveled the border between Samaria and Galilee. "Jesus, Master, have pity on us." After Jesus healed them, only one man later came back to Him, fell on His feet, and thanked Him. "Jesus asked 'Were not all ten cleansed? Where are the other nine?" (Luke 16:27)

Are we among the nine lepers who don't return to give thanks, or are we the one who does? The secret of happiness lies in our response to the question.

Prayer: Dear Lord God, sometimes we are like Your people who wandered in the wilderness for forty years and were always whining and complaining even when You were fulfilling their needs. Give us grateful hearts that return to You often to praise and thank You. Amen.

40

Too Busy

Luke 10:38-42 At the home of Martha and Mary

Luke 10:41&42 "Martha, Martha," the Lord answered, "you are worried and upset about many things, but only one thing is needed."

Shopping and mopping, baking and shaking, shining and polishing, I am so busy today! Company is coming and I've so much to do! Too busy to sit and relax a while, when there is so much to do! Company is coming and we must put our best foot forward. No quiet time today to spend with my Lord!

Sometimes I can really sympathize with Martha who was undoubtedly scurrying about to prepare a tasty meal for Jesus who was a guest in their home. And while she was wiping her brow over a hot oven, her sister Mary was indolently sitting at the feet of Jesus, visiting with Him, giving Him her rapt attention. Exasperated, Martha went to the living room and in essence said, "Jesus, don't you care how hard I'm working? Tell my sister to get into the kitchen and help me!"

But Jesus gently rebuffed her. He told Martha that she was careful and worried and upset about too many things. He championed Mary by saying that she was pursuing better priorities– things of spiritual and eternal consequence!

Even when company is coming, I must remember Martha and take time for reading the Word and sitting at the feet of Jesus. Even when company isn't coming, I need to invite Jesus into my home and heart daily.

The Apostle Paul writes about the things that perchance could separate us from Christ in the eighth chapter of Romans. He mentions such dire things as persecution, famine, nakedness, dangers of all kinds, and affirms that they can not come between us and Christ. Neither heights, nor depths, nor angels nor demons shall separate us from "the love of God that is in Christ Jesus our Lord."

But sometimes I have to wonder if I, like Martha, don't separate myself from Him in my busyness, by inattention to what is *really* important in life! I can hear Jesus saying, "Marcia, Marcia, you are worried and bothered about many things, come and rest awhile with Me!"

Prayer: Dear Lord Jesus, how precious to sit at your feet and be blessed by your Words and your unfathomable love. Keep me from being so busy that I "separate" myself from knowing You better and growing stronger in You. Thank You for the wonderful promises, encouragement, and refreshment that I receive in quiet times with You. Amen.

41

Call Waiting

I Peter 3:12 For the eyes of the Lord are on the righteous and his ears are attentive to their prayer, but the face of the Lord is against those who do evil.

Psalm 116: 1&2 I love the Lord, for he heard my voice; he heard my cry for mercy. Because he turned his ear to me, I will call on him as long as I live.

"Just a moment, I have another call coming in...I'll have to put you on hold." Your telephone call to a friend or associate has been interrupted, and now you sit tapping your fingers on the table waiting to continue your call. How does it make you feel, this marvel of modern technology which gives someone else the ability to interrupt your conversation? It's as if that third person may be more important and interesting so you are abruptly put on hold. To me this particular development of the techo age seems almost rude. If the carrier of such a service is an emergency worker or is a volunteer firefighter or is the President of the United States, this would certainly be acceptable. But for the rest of those incoming calls, just wait your turn, please!

Aren't you glad that God doesn't employ the "call waiting"

feature or put us "on hold" when we pray to Him? Isn't it wonderful that the phone lines are always open to Him, day or night, and His ears are always "attentive to our prayers"? And we know He is a very busy God for millions of calls ascend to Him every moment, but He takes them all. He doesn't put us on hold and pipe some heavenly harp music into our ear as we wait interminably.

What a marvelous God we have who has the spiritual technology to hear all our prayers at all times! He welcomes our phone calls, waits longingly for us to dial Him up. We are urged to pray without ceasing and in all circumstances. (I Thess. 5:17) We are enjoined to ask, seek, and knock. (Luke 11:9)

The Lord knows our voices, and He is always happy to hear from us when we call upon Him. He wants us to just call and chat anytime, without interruption. And in times of emergency, He is always open to our 911 calls. "Call upon me in the day of trouble; I will deliver you, and you will honor me." (Ps. 50:15)

Whatsmore, our calls are never "out of range." Call Him from Pikes Peak, or Death Valley, or the moon, and He will hear. Jonah called from the bowels of a whale in the depths of the sea. He later testified that his prayers were heard: "In my distress I called to the Lord, and he answered me. From the depths of the grave I called for help, and you listened to my cry." (Jonah 2:1)

Another reason to call our Lord is just to thank Him for his "goodness and faithfulness" (Ps. 100:5) and to sing our praises unto Him.

The phone lines are always open to our Lord and there are no limited hours or days for your call, no "over-minutes" charges, and no "calls waiting"!

*Prayer: Hello, God, it's me and I'm just calling to say thank you for all the calls you've taken from me, however urgent or however routine. Sometimes You say, "no"; sometimes "yes"; and sometimes You say "wait," but You **always** give me Your ear and I am so very grateful! In Jesus, Amen.*

42

The Baby Jesus Has Been Misplaced

2 Cor. 4:4 The God of this age has blinded the minds of unbelievers, so they cannot see the gospel of the glory of Christ, who is the image of God.

What if we opened the newspaper to the classifieds one December morning and found this ad:

"LOST: A baby known as Jesus. Perhaps in a department store in the Christmas rush. Perhaps in the tinsel of holiday decorations, or in Santa's little red house on the courthouse lawn. The babe was last seen before the outbreak of feasting and merrymaking at parties. Search under mountains of coats in restaurants, clubs, and homes. Consider whether he was misplaced under heaps of crumpled wrapping paper and ribbons, forgotten in the flurry of practicing the pageant, or stuffing the stockings. This adorable, glowing baby, filled with Life and Peace and Truth, has been misplaced by many celebrants. REWARD! Above all monetary measure to the finder.

This child is a priceless gift from a loving Father, and without him all else is lost!"

But the "God of this age" would undoubtedly blind our eyes even to such a plea, buried as it would be in newspapers among all the seasonal come-ons and advertisements.

Who is the "God of this age" (see 2 Cor. 4:4 above) who has blinded us, not only the unbelievers, but the believers as well, as we often get side-tracked during the Christmas season?

The Message Bible terms the "God of this age" as the "fashionable god of darkness." Perhaps the excessive commercialization of Christmas makes us want to do what is expected of us in the eyes of the world, to do what is "fashionable."

Perhaps we get mired down because the "god" of tradition calls to us: we "always" make at least nine dozen cookies. We "always" host a big dinner with ham, cranberries, pecan pies, and all the trimmings. We "always" brave the crowds to shop for gifts for everyone including the postman, the barber, the beauty shop operator, the neighbors, great aunts and uncles and numerous other extended family members. We "always" decorate a ten-foot tree, hoist Santa, his sleigh and the reindeer to the roof of the house.

Meanwhile, the One whom we are celebrating gets lost in the hustle and bustle. As the cash registers ring up the extravagance of buying gifts and decorations and foodstuffs, the mass of people are joining in a revelry that often has little to do with the birth of Jesus. Even our believer's eyes can be blinded by the glitter of the season, and we lose sight of the glorious child who is the TRUE Light of the World!

Let's not misplace Him in all the hoopla and wrappings of the season! Let's collect the "Reward" offered in the newspaper ad written above, and be ever mindful of the magnificent reason for our celebration.

Prayer: Father of the Holy Child, we rejoice in your most wondrous gift. Help us not to get side-tracked this Christmas season, but let it be a time of true worship and adoration of our Savior, Jesus Christ. Amen.

43

Sportsmanship of the Highest Order

Matt. 7:12 In everything, do to others what you would have them do to you, for this sums up the Law and the Prophets.

Phil. 2:15 ....so that you may become blameless and pure, children of God without fault in a crooked and depraved generation, in which you shine like stars in the universe.

We live in a very competitive society. Children are taught at a very young age to "go out there and be the best." The sports arena is especially competitive for players, coaches, and fans. It's a "win-at-any-cost" society that often leaves sportsmanship in the dust.

But here is a case where "do unto others as you would have them do unto you" took precedence over the final score. Gainesville State School was a maximum correctional facility for boys 12 to 19 and they were scheduled to play against Grapevine Faith Christian School, a nine times state championship team. The Grapevine coach, Kris Hogan, could have used this opportunity to humiliate the prison team. Instead, he looked upon it as an opportunity to demonstrate Christ's love. Realizing the Gainesville team would play with empty stands on their side, he sent out letters to the Grapevine parents asking them to sit on the prisoners' side and printed up rosters with the player's names for more personal support. He even divided up the cheerleaders and asked half of them to go to the Gainesville side and root for them. Grapevine *did* win the game 33 to 14, but it wasn't the massacre it could have been. Then as the Gainesville players were escorted back to their bus by uniformed police officers, another surprise awaited them. Each of the boys was handed a burger, fries, and a Coke from the host school.

"Before everybody went their separate ways, the losing coach grabbed Coach Hogan by the shoulders. He looked him in the eye and said, 'You'll never know what your people did for these kids tonight. You'll never, ever know.'" (From a column by Pastor Ken Klaus in "The Lutheran Layman," May-June 2012)

It was Christ's love and "do unto others" that led Coach Hogan to show "mercy" instead of "muscle" over the Gainesville team that day. And surely those ripples of kindness flowed far out from the arena to bless, not only the recipients, but all who participated in this act of sportsmanship of the highest order.

As the oft quoted poem declares: "For when the One Great Scorer comes To write against your name, He marks-not that you won or lost– But how you played the game."–Grantland Rice

Prayer: Christ, our Champion, our Coach, and our Lord, help us to play the game according to Your divine will, and inspire all of us to be Your shining stars. Amen.

44

Don't Cry

Luke 7:13 When the Lord saw her, his heart went out to her and he said, "Don't cry."

"Don't cry," Jesus said to the bereaved and distraught mother of an only son when Jesus happened to meet her and the funeral cortege at the town gate of Nain. He saw the agony on her face, spiritually perceived her deep grief, and He was filled with compassion for her. Not only was her mother's heart wrenched by the death of her beloved son, in addition, she had lost her means of support. In those days before Social Security, she would have been at the mercy of whoever might give her a handout. "Don't cry," Jesus said and within moments He had raised her son from the dead.

It is interesting that though Jesus tells the widow not to cry, He, Himself, cried when He heard of the death of his friend Lazarus. Thus, the shortest verse in the Bible, "Jesus wept," (John 11:35) concerned the death of one dearly loved as a brother. In this case, our Lord, knowing that He had the power to restore life, still reacted in a very human way.

One wonders if the tears of Jesus were not also for the human condition, that because of sin, man must die. (Romans 6:23) It was a compassion that took Him ultimately to the cross.

A few years ago I heard a mortician give a speech about his profession. He said that he liked helping survivors at this most fragile and vulnerable time of their lives. He also said that the hardest funerals were those where the mourners had no hope of an after-life. The most gratifying were those where the mourners believed in Christ and had an assurance that they would see their loved one again. The tears of Christians do not have the bitter sting of those who mourn in hopeless despair.

"Don't cry." Jesus still speaks those words to all of us. "I have come to rescue you from the power of death. Don't cry! I have gone to prepare a mansion in heaven for you, and one day I will gather you unto myself and my Father will wipe away all your tears." (See John 3:16, John 14:2 and Rev. 7:17)

Prayer: Precious Jesus, You have such a great heart of understanding and love for us, a love so undeserved. By Your grace we can face the death of our saved loved ones and our own death with confidence. Thank You for Your unfailing compassion and comfort as You lead us through the valley of death. Amen.

45

Water of Life

John 7:37-38 On the last and greatest day of the Feast, Jesus stood and said in a loud voice, "If a man is thirsty, let him come to me and drink. Whoever believes in me, as the Scripture has said, streams of living water will flow from within him."

We take water for granted. In most places in America we have bountiful supplies of life- giving water, and everyday, without thinking much about it, we let the faucets splash forth clean water which we use for a multitude of purposes. Water for cooking, for brushing our teeth, washing our clothes, scrubbing our floors, washing our cars, watering our livestock, pets, and gardens, and first and foremost– for drinking! How blessed we are!

But sometimes areas within our country have known seasons of drought. For instance, the dust bowl days of the '20's in the Midwest, and more recently, the drought in the Southwest. The state of Texas was among those devastated by a shortage of water in 2011. For seven long record-setting months the rain didn't fall. The landscape became parched and scaly. Pastures dried up; cattle herds had to be thinned or dispersed of as there was no water to provide them food and sustenance. Crops failed; the cotton output was dismal. Water was rationed in the cities as reservoirs dried up. The state known for its lovely blue-bonnet flowers turned brown and barren. Thankfully, the rains came in the winter and spring of 2011-2012 and the bluebonnets are once more flourishing in copious bouquets along the roadsides of Texas, a symbol of new life and hope.

There are places on the planet where the people struggle endlessly with the lack of water. In Ethiopia, the women walk miles to fill tankards with water and then carry the heavy burdens on their backs to their homes. Sometimes this daily trek involves many hours of drudgery. We can share the wonderful blessing of water by giving to charities which will provide for the digging of wells in some of these arid lands. How those African women must rejoice when clear, precious water bubbles up almost at their doorsteps. What a simple and yet life-affirming gift– a fresh-water well!

But there is another kind of water that is imperative to share– and that is the Water of Life, Jesus Christ Himself. Just as we humans need H2O to physically survive, we need spiritual water for our thirsty and famishing souls. This is the water of the Holy Spirit flowing into our hearts as in faith we receive Jesus as our Lord and Savior so we can survive eternally with Him. Jesus invites everyone unto Himself, and in John 7 assures as that if we believe in Him, "streams of living water will flow from us." Are we willing to share this most vital gift with the nations?

In the book of Revelation, John speaks of a vision of heaven which he was permitted to see. "Then the angel showed me the river of the water of life, as clear as crystal, flowing from the throne of God and the Lamb down the middle of the great street of the city. On each side of the river stood the tree of life, bearing twelve crops of fruit, yielding its fruit every month.

And the leaves of the tree are for the healing of the nations."
(Rev. 22:1&2)

All the streams from all who believe are tributaries from this great river of life. How blessed we are!

Prayer: Our God of Abundant Goodness, enthroned by the river of life, we thank and praise You for the great resource of water which You provide on this planet, and we also praise and thank you for Jesus who gives us the water which bubbles up into life eternal. Amen.

46

The Four-Eyed Fish

Phil. 3:20 But our citizenship is in heaven. And we eagerly await a Savior from there, the Lord Jesus Christ...

Phil. 1: 21 & 22a For me to live is Christ and to die is gain. If I am to go on living in the body, this will mean fruitful labor for me...

Christians could be compared to a "four-eyed fish," a species that has been endowed by its Creator with large bulging eyes that have a remarkable capacity–they can see above the water and below the water at the same time! The upper part of each bulbous eye contains an air lens and the bottom part contains a water lens. The four sets of lenses perform as natural bifocals so that the fish is able to see the upper-world above the water, and the under-world below the water simultaneously.

In many ways we are like this tropical, minnow-like fish. First and foremost, we are citizens of heaven who keep our upwards gaze upon Christ, and yet we must also be aware of the planet upon which we trod. We are not *of* this world, and yet we are *in* this world, so it is necessary that we look for opportunities to serve while we exist bodily in this world.

Even though we are only foreigners and travelers through

this land, we need to have our earthly eyes wide open to ways we can serve our Master. There is hunger, poverty, loneliness, and distress all around us. Let us not be like those whose heads are so stuck in the clouds of Glory-land, that they are of no earthly value to Christ. St. Paul declared that if he had his druthers, he would like to be living above with Christ, but if God willed for him to live on earth a while longer, then he would use his time in "fruitful labor" for others.

It was an interesting reversal in the life of Paul of Tarsus who went from persecuting Christians to becoming one of the staunchest of them. When Jesus spoke to him on the road to Damascus, Paul was struck blind in a dramatic conversion experience. He eventually regained his eyesight, but more importantly, he became a new man endowed with spiritual vision as he aspired to become more Christlike. (See Acts 9) He was bound by the words of Jesus, "Blessed are those who hunger and thirst for righteousness for they will be filled. Blessed are the merciful, for they will be shown mercy. Blessed are the pure in heart, for they will *see* God." (Matt. 5: 6-8, Emphasis mine)

And we, also, will *see* God through a prism of blessings, if we employ our bifocal vision as we travel through this underworld, looking for ways to serve Him, all the while keeping the upper lens of our eyes focused on the Kingdom of Heaven where our true citizenship resides.

Prayer: Glorious God, we rejoice in our citizenship in heaven which you have bestowed upon us through our dear Savior, Jesus Christ. Help us to keep our eyes upon You, as we also look for ways to serve You on this earth. Amen.

47

Good Is in the Details

Proverbs 3:6 In all thy ways acknowledge him, and he shall direct thy paths. (KJV)

Phil. 4:6 Be careful for nothing; but in everything by prayer and supplication with thanksgiving let your requests be made known unto God. (KJV)

I Thess. 5: 17&18 Pray continually; give thanks in all circumstances, for this is God's will for you in Christ Jesus.

When I first glanced at the colorful sign spread across the side of a Pepperidge Farms delivery truck, I thought it said, "God is in the details." But as I approached the truck which was parked on the lot of the local grocery store, and as my eyes took in the huge, mouth-watering chocolate chip cookie illustration, I re-read the words...Oh!.. "*Good* is in the details"! Details like premium ingredients, real butter, fresh eggs and lots of smooth, rich chocolate bits, no doubt. It's the small things that go into baking a good product that make a big difference in the end result.

Likewise, it's the details of our lives that all mixed together produce a pleasant or distasteful experience. God is in the details, from the time we get up in the morning and all through the small moments which make up the substance of our days. And since He values our lives, there is nothing so trivial or insignificant that we should not ask for His guidance and help.

Does that mean such things as opening up a parking space for us on a crowded street, asking for His help in finding good sale prices as we shop, pleading for a win by our favorite team? Some people are scandalized that a busy God who has the machinery of a universe to attend to and heavy, consequential matters on His mind should be bothered with our trivialities.

But doesn't He advise us in His Word to call upon Him in *all* matters which concern us, to worry about nothing, to pray continually–and give thanks always. To be in constant touch with Him for He cares for us and knows that details are important. It must please our loving Father when we want to communicate with Him, and demonstrate in prayer our reliance upon Him. It is His delight to give us His loving attention at all times and in all things.

Taste and see that the Lord is good...He nourishes us, protects us, guides us, loves us with a love unimaginable.

Life is good when we trust Him for the details...even better than a huge, oven-fresh chocolate chip cookie, like the one pictured on the side of the Pepperidge Farm delivery truck!

Prayer: Our Gracious Lord, as we look about us, we see the attention to detail You put into Creation from the fine veins on a leaf to the intricate design on a butterfly's wings. Thank You for being a loving God who is also caring about even the smallest details of our lives. Praise to You! Amen.

48

From the Hand of God

Ps. 145: 15&16 The eyes of all look to you, and you give them their food at the proper time. You open your hand and satisfy the desires of every living thing.

Exodus 16: 13a That evening quail came and covered the camp....

It wasn't "pheasant under glass," but that quail must have really tasted good to the meat-starved Israelites after wandering for many days in the desert after their escape from slavery in Egypt.

They had grumbled to Moses and Aaron as they thought longingly about the pots of meat they had left behind in Egypt. On this journey the Lord had fed them faithfully with manna, "bread from heaven," which they had picked up off the ground every morning, but the nomads craved something more succulent and savory. Imagine their glad cries when they heard the flutter of wings, and a covey of quail flew right into their camp. (See Exodus, chapter 16) Surely they were happier campers when fires were lit, and the smell of roasting birds made their mouths salivate.

The Psalmist declared: "The eyes of all look to you, and you give them their food at the proper time." (Ps. 145:15)

Donald Lienemann was a B-17 navigator who was captured and taken to Stalag Luft I, a German prison camp during World War II. During his time there he lost over fifty pounds on the lean rations that he and his fellow prisoners were granted. He was especially thankful for the food made available to them by the American Red Cross, but in March of 1945 those rations came to a halt. The packages had been intercepted and looted by Germans and the American soldiers faced starvation that especially grim month. But then something amazing happened!

During one bitterly cold night a windstorm with snow flurries arose, and a cloud of birds attempted to fly– something rarely done by birds at night. They became blinded by the strong floodlights surrounding the perimeter of the camp, and they flew headlong into the barracks, thudding and thumping to their deaths. The next morning the men rubbed their eyes and looked out onto God's provision, dead and frozen birds– some ducks, but mostly starlings and sparrows.

They went out, gathered them up, dressed them and as Donald said, "ate heartily that evening."

Despite being surrounded by barbed wire on four sides and heavily guarded, God saw to it that they got something to eat. They were very thankful for, indeed, in a miraculous way God had opened His hand and satisfied their hunger.

A few weeks later, the Russians arrived to liberate them. The Allies were very generous, procuring flour, bread and other edibles for them. They even drove in a hundred head of milk cows which provided the soldiers with milk and steaks. Donald Lienemann from Papillion, NE, wrote in his book, "Miracles Do Happen," (Morris Publishing, Kearney, NE, 2003) that the incident with the birds "points out a very good lesson, namely, that as long as you have faith you will be fed, regardless of how it may come about."

Whether it is quail, pheasant, sparrows, steaks, or simply manna, you will be fed. And God uses many means, including birds flying in freezing windstorms, the Red Cross, and even you and me to accomplish His will of feeding the hungry.

Prayer: Precious Lord, thank You for feeding us daily from Your hand. Thank You for the miracles of quail in the desert and birds in the prison camp. Help us to respond to hunger in the world today. Amen.

49

When Confronting a Large Task

Ps. 46:11 The Lord Almighty is with us; the God of Jacob is our fortress.

Neh. 8:10b ...for the joy of the Lord is your strength.

Have you ever had a monumental task set before you and wondered how on earth you would accomplish it? We can take a cue from Nehemiah who set out to rebuild the wall around Jerusalem in 445 B.C., and despite the odds for any ordinary man, he was successful through prayer and an unwavering confidence in God.

Nehemiah was a cupbearer for Artaxerxes, king of Persia, but when he heard of the destruction in his Jewish homeland, he was overcome with grief and anguish. For four months he prayed, and when the opportunity came, he asked the king for permission to go back and build the wall. The initial prayer as recorded in Nehemiah, chapter one, is considered by many to be one of the most moving prayers in the Old Testament. It contains praise, confession of the collective sins of his people, and petitions for God's help in this undertaking (a task which had undoubtedly been laid upon his heart by God Himself).

Nehemiah as it turns out was a very capable leader and

the right man for the job. When he returned to his homeland he was able to inspire the Jews who still lived there to become involved with this formidable task. He was a good organizer, making various priests and families responsible for rebuilding certain gates and portions of the wall. He gave them respect and in the book of Nehemiah he writes the names of all the volunteers who came forth.

As could be expected, Satan attempted to interfere with the rebuilding of the fortress around the Holy City, and tried to discourage Nehemiah so he would give up and go home. Enemies taunted him at first, and eventually tried to attack the workers. Even some of his so- called friends tried to lure him into traps to discredit and waylay him. (See Nehemiah 6)

But Nehemiah would not be deterred or tricked. He stood strong, drenching the project with his prayers. He eventually had to separate the men (and some women who helped) into two forces, one to build and the other to be armed guards against enemies who threatened to assault them. Some of the people even worked with a construction tool in one hand and a weapon in the other. Nehemiah persevered as he prayed, "O God, strengthen my hands." (Neh. 6:9)

It was an arduous task. Nehemiah and his crews worked day and night, but in the end the Lord gave them success and they finished rebuilding the wall and the gates in 52 days, an amazing accomplishment!

But building a physical wall wasn't enough— Nehemiah knew that God had allowed the destruction of the wall by Judah's enemies many years ago because of their sins. Now it was time for a spiritual rebuilding. He and the priest Ezra called for many days of the reading of God's Word— the Law— which led to repentance and revival among the Jewish people.

Nehemiah is a man to admire— a role model for all of us

who struggle with a task that God has apportioned unto us. It is through faith and prayer that success is possible, even against all odds.

Prayer: Our Father in heaven, we praise You and give You the glory for what You did through Your willing servant, Nehemiah. Speak also to our hearts and work through our hands to accomplish Your will. We turn our tasks over to You, and ask Your blessings upon our efforts. In the name of Jesus, Amen.

50

Out-of-Control Drivers

Proverbs 16:32 Better to be patient than powerful; better to have self-control than to conquer a city. (NLT)

When "tin lizzies" first made their appearances on the roadways of our nation and caused the teams of horses pulling carriages to get skittish and bolt, it undoubtedly produced some of our first occurrences of "road rage." As more and more vehicles share our highways these days, there are more occasions when tempers flare, and road anger escalates. These unbridled outbursts of emotion can lead to wrecked cars and even bodily harm.

For instance, on Highway Interstate 95 in Virginia in 2010, a "ticked-off" driver of a silver Jaguar ended up firing 13 shots at a dump truck that had, perhaps carelessly, merged into the traffic from a side street. The two vehicles angrily jockeyed back and forth through lanes of traffic for several miles, pushing each other until the Jaguar scraped against a wall. That's when the driver jumped out of his dented car and fired a gun into the departing truck. The Jaguar driver's two-year-old daughter was in the car at the time. Luckily, no one was physically hurt, but the whole situation could have been disastrous.

In all our interactions in life, whether with strangers or with familiar people, it is important to maintain self-control.

Perhaps that is why St. Paul so often mentioned its value in his various epistles. In the first chapter of the book of Titus, Paul exhorts Titus to appoint elders in Crete that are not "quick tempered," but "self-controlled," among other notable qualities (See verses 7 & 8). Paul continues with advice for Titus in how to teach righteous living to the followers: for the older men, they should be urged to be "temperate" ... "self-controlled" and "sound in faith," (See Titus 2:2). For the older women, they also, along with other worthy qualities, should be "self-controlled," verse 4. "Similarly, encourage the young men to be self-controlled," verse 6. The second chapter concludes: "It (the Grace of God) teaches us to say 'No' to worldly passions, and to live self-controlled, upright and godly lives in this present age..," verse 12. Five times Paul exhorts "self-control" within the first two chapters of Titus, as recorded in the NIV translation of the Bible.

Though they may not have had "road rage" in Paul's day (but then again, maybe those camels and donkeys did have flare-ups among their drivers!) Paul understood how important self-control is and mentioned it as one of the fruits of the Spirit in Galatians 5:22. Out-of- control passions can lead to wrecked cars, wrecked lives, and/or wrecked relationships on the "road of life." Passage will go so much more smoothly if we can exercise self-control at all times.

Prayer: Our heavenly Father, cause the fruits of Your Spirit to take root and grow in us. Help us to manage our tempers and passions so that we may live Holy and Godly lives. In the name of Jesus we pray. Amen.

51

Just Say Thank You

Ps. 50:23 Giving thanks is a sacrifice that truly honors me. If you keep to my path, I will reveal to you the Salvation of God. (NLT)

Ps. 118:1 Give thanks to the Lord, for he is good! (NLT)

A grandfather and his granddaughter were at odds. In fact, he had threatened to disown her because the twenty-something law graduate had not thanked him for a Christmas gift of $25.00. The son of the grandfather, who was also the father of the neglectful daughter, wrote to "Ask Amy" for her advice on how to heal the breach.

The columnist replied, "...for goodness sake, cut the guy (the grandfather) a break and just say thank you! It is rude, tacky, ungracious and wrong not to thank someone for a gift. And it takes two minutes."* Just two minutes to restore a relationship.

It is rude and ungracious not to acknowledge a gift, even if we don't especially like the gift, or if we just don't want to bother with the formality. Jesus once healed ten lepers, but only one was gracious enough to come back later, throw himself at the feet of Jesus, and thank Him. (Interestingly, the only one with the decency to express his gratitude was a lowly Samaritan.) Then, "Jesus asked, 'Were not all ten cleansed? Where are the other nine?'" (Luke 17:17) The foreigner (Samaritan) gave the sacrifice which honors God. (See Ps. 50:23 written above)

Are we willing to sacrifice the breath and time it takes to say "Thank you"? A telephone call, an e-mail, a note are simple ways to convey appreciation. It really isn't that hard or time- consuming.

If a child is well-trained, he will usually know that saying "Thank You" is just plain good etiquette, even if it isn't always in earnest. Good manners dictates that it is "rude and tacky" not to say the simple, yet magical words, "Thank you."

Later in life, those children, hopefully, will transpose what was perhaps said by rote to genuine and sincere appreciation. I once read about a retired schoolteacher who was feeling lonely and useless. One day she received a letter in the mail– a beautiful expression of gratitude from a former student. He wrote of how special she was to him and how much she had impacted his life for good. Tearfully, the old teacher said that it was the first and only time that one, out of the hundreds of children she taught, had come back and said, "Thank you"!

Think how much our heavenly Father who gives us all things must appreciate our thanks and praise. I confess that I do not do it enough myself. Psalm 100:4 exhorts us: "Enter into his gates with thanksgiving, and into his courts with praise; give thanks to him and praise his name." (KJV) When we come to say "Thank you" to our heavenly Father, we are ushered through the sweet-smelling courtyards of heaven and into the very throne room of God!

Such a simple, easy, and often neglected way to enhance our relationship with our Lord!

And such an easy way that a granddaughter could heal her relationship with a loved one– by just saying "Thank you"!

Prayer: Dear Father in Heaven, I enter now Your court-yard with praise for a jillion things, but most especially for Your love, and the gift of Your Dear Son! Thank You! Thank You! Amen.

* "Ask Amy" column, Amy Dickinson, "Lincoln Journal Star," June 28, 2012.

52

Riches in Secret Places

Col. 2:3b ...so that they may have the full riches of complete understanding in order that they may know the mystery of God, namely Christ, in whom are hidden all the treasures of wisdom and knowledge.

Is. 45:3 I will give the treasures of darkness, riches stored in secret places so that you may know I am the Lord, the God of Israel, who summons you by name.

What if your children were hungry and yet stored away in a locked box was a great treasure that you could sell and buy food for your children. Would you do it?

Jeannette Walls writes of growing up in poverty in her memoir, "The Glass Castle" (Scribner, 2005). She and her three siblings often went hungry. When the refrigerator was nearly bare, they grabbed chunks of margarine and ate it. They scavenged in dumpsters for anything edible. At school, Jeannette seldom ate lunch, often sitting in a stall in the restroom to escape notice. When other students would throw away such things as bologna sandwiches or apples in the restroom trash can, she would sneak out of her stall and stash it away to eat later.

Once she and her brother tried to eat pokeweed which grew behind their house. It was awfully bitter so they tried boiling it, but it was sour and stringy and made their tongues itch for days afterward. Their fanciful mother who deemed herself an artist and above mundane work, and their alcoholic father were too proud to apply for food stamps so their children went hungry.

One day as Jeannette and her brother scouted about for food, they found a two-carat diamond ring in the dirt. After their mother had it appraised, she decided to keep it and wear it for... "it would be good for her self-esteem." Meanwhile, the father kept making promises he couldn't keep, like building a castle out of glass for his family to live in.

At the age of seventeen, Jeannette escaped to New York and became successful despite her background. Her parents later followed her, and refusing to work or accept help from Jeannette, became homeless squatters in run-down tenements.

Supposedly, long ago, her mother had inherited some land in Texas, but all through the years Mrs. Walls was very evasive about it. Perhaps it was just a few acres of dried-up, cracked desert as far as she knew, but as an adult, Jeannette found out that it was a valuable piece of real estate. "I was thunderstruck. All those years in Welch (West Virginia) with no food, no coal, no plumbing, and Mom had been sitting on land worth a million dollars!" she wrote.

Holding on to the diamond ring... holding on to the land had been more important to Mrs. Walls than feeding her children. The Lord is not so stingy with us, his children. He says, "I will give you the treasures of darkness..." (See Is. 45:3 as written above). Out of His storehouse of riches, He will feed our hungry souls with the knowledge of Christ and an abundance of spiritual blessings. From the darkness of our troubles and turmoil here on earth, we need to flee to His castles of Light and radiant truth so that we can feast on His promises.

Prayer: Our Beneficent Lord, we thank You for the promises You have given us in the Bible. Your greatest desire is for us to walk in Your ways and unearth the abundance of Your riches which You have given us in Christ. As we are filled and our spirits hunger no more, help us to generously share those hidden riches with others. Hallelujah! Amen.

53

Why Are We Here?

Genesis 2:7 And the Lord God formed man from the dust of the ground and breathed into his nostrils the breath of life, and man became a living being.

The age-old question is WHY? Why did God create man knowing even before He molded and made him, that man would fall. Knowing all this, God created a being that possessed a mind, a conscience, and a free will, instead of a robot. And even before He breathed life into the first man's nostrils, He knew that man would sin!

So why did He create us?– He could have saved Himself a lot of disappointment and headaches if He had stopped his creative splurge with say– the zebras! Now there is a beautiful and noble animal– why not call it a day, and stop right there!

God didn't really need us– He is all-sufficient! In the Garden of Eden, God brought the animals to Adam and gave him the task of naming them. "So the man gave names to all the livestock, the birds of the air and all the beasts of the field." (Gen. 2:20) But we all would surely agree that the God who master-minded the amazing and varied creation of the animals didn't really need any help in naming them. Perhaps he just wanted Adam to feel useful.

"I believe God brought us into the world to serve Him," said a man in our Bible study group recently. But if God wanted a servant, He could have stopped with a German shepherd dog, which probably would have been more loyal and steadfast.

"He created us to enjoy and appreciate the earth that He had fashioned. He wanted a cheering section!" responded another intrepid study-mate. But the all-powerful, all-knowing, all-sufficient God of the universe surely didn't *need* ego-stroking.

In researching this question, I have read that the Bible doesn't really say why God created mankind. But somehow, I hold with James Weldon Johnson who wrote "The Creation."

This powerful poem resounds with the cadence of a Negro spiritual as verse after verse describes the Lord bringing forth sun and stars, rivers and lakes, fishes and fowls, beasts and birds and finally-- "He looked on his world With all its living things/ and God said: 'I'm lonely still...'/

And he thought and thought, Till he thought:/ 'I'll make me a man!'"

Who can prove whether God was really all that lonely, but we are told that He created us in His image, with a soul, and through that soul He could commune with us. Like a benevolent father who enjoys giving to his children, He wants us to delight in the world He created. For Adam and Eve who walked with the Lord in the cool of the evening in the Garden of Eden– before their fall into sin– the communion must have been extremely blissful.

Then sin destroyed that perfect relationship. However, God wouldn't give up on us; He loved these man-creatures so much that He sent His only begotten Son to redeem us. "His unchanging plan has always been to adopt us into his own family by bringing us to Himself through Jesus Christ. And this gave him great pleasure." (Ephesians 1:5 NLT)

I believe that God created us for a deep companionship of the soul which He couldn't attain through a zebra, lovely and exotic as they are!

Prayer: Dear Father God, how pleasant it is to walk in the garden with You, to enjoy Your beautiful creation, and most of all, to know the pleasures of Your divine fellowship. You created each of us with a great hole in our heart that can only be filled by You. Thanks and praise to You for sending Your Son to restore peace with You! Alleluia! Amen.

54

Off to Work We Go

Ecclesiastes 5:19 Moreover, when God gives any man wealth and possessions, and enables him to enjoy them, to accept his lot and be happy in his work— this is a gift from God.

"I hear America singing, the varied carols I hear; Those of mechanics— each one singing his, as it should be, blithe and strong; The carpenter singing his... the boatman singing his... the shoemaker, the wood-cutter...the delicious singing of the mother—or the young wife at work—or of the girl sewing or washing—Each singing what belongs to her, and to none else." These lines and phrases were excerpted from a poem by Walt Whitman in which he extols the grandeur of industrious Americans. "I Hear America Singing" is a lovely carol celebrating the vibrant joy of people at work in the young democracy.

It surely is a "gift of God" if one can immerse his or her talents and passions into daily work that is rewarding and fulfilling. Sadly, many people plod from paycheck to paycheck in a job that is to them toilsome drudgery. Certainly every vocation has its "ups and downs" and there will be times of stress and frustration in all callings. However, if one sings as he works, as in Whitman's poem, he adds a "joie de vivre" to the workplace and to his own heart.

Sometimes what it takes is a change of attitude toward one's work, asking God to reveal the worthiness of your vocation whether it be a doctor, a nurse, a farmer, a teacher, a tradesman, a factory worker, a sales clerk, or a janitor. All work has dignity if it is done unto the Lord.

On the other hand, a persistent unhappiness on the job may be a signal to search out a new work path. This may entail more education to achieve a "long-dreamed-of" career, or it may mean daring to seek different opportunities. In these days, many people, through no fault of their own, have lost their jobs because of downsizing, which in turn has led them to discover new and satisfying vocations.

Certainly, we humans were created for work. It is a way to utilize our talents and serve each other, as well as God. To lie around without purpose would be numbing to brain and body.

Down through the centuries it is work that has kept this world humming. Life would be empty without it.

As Theodore Roosevelt once said: "Far and away the best prize that life has to offer is the chance to work hard at work worth doing." I'm sure Walt Whitman would have agreed.

Prayer: Dear Father in Heaven, even from the time You gave Adam the work of naming the animals in the garden of Eden, You knew our need to be usefully employed. Thank You for work and the fruits of our labors which You give us to enjoy. Hear us now as we sing our thanks and praise unto You. Amen.

55

Expelling the Flotsam

Phil. 3:13b & 14 But one thing I do: Forgetting what is behind and straining toward what is ahead, I press on toward the goal to win the prize for which God has called me heavenward in Christ Jesus.

One morning I awoke early and lay in those gray hours before dawn reflecting on past slights and resentments. As one unhappy memory slid into another, it became an unending litany of woes. A student who long ago had hurt my feelings so deeply, a betrayal by an old friend, and on and on, the surging reminders of skewed relationships, regrets, failures, embarrassments, kept flooding forth from some muddy caverns deep within my mind. Why? Where was all this coming from?

"Why are you downcast, O my soul? Why so disturbed within me? Put your hope in God, for I will yet praise him, my Savior and my God." (Ps. 42:11) I chastised myself for letting the flotsam and jetsam, the debris, of the past spoil this fresh new day. All of this should be left behind as I move forward in faith. With St. Paul I desire to "forget the past and look forward to what lies ahead." (My paraphrase of the verse above as written in The Living Bible.)

Somehow the words of a song by the Beatles, of all unlikely places, eases into my consciousness: "Let It Be" by Paul

McCartney. His mother's name was Mary and she died when he was fourteen years old. In ensuing years, at the height of the band's success, tensions grew among the four musicians. Paul, troubled and upset, went to bed one night and had a lovely dream in which his mother appeared to him. Paul later said that they had a nice visit which was such a blessing to him, and she left him with the words, "It will be all right, just let it be."

"Let it be," so quaintly British, and yet so universally true. It is time for me to leave the flotsam behind, get out of bed, and move on.

This morning is a clean slate that the Lord has given me. Forgiving and forgiven, I can cast nettling thoughts aside and step out into this brand new day without being weighed down by the flotsam of the past. "Because of the Lord's great love, we are not consumed, for his compassions never fail. They are new every morning; great is your faithfulness." (Lamentations 3: 22&23)

Prayer: My Faithful Lord, help me to forget those things that weigh down my soul and hold me back from living joyfully in You. Let me not squander this new day living in the past, but spend it well, pressing on in Your Spirit. Amen.

56

The Name That Saves

Matthew 1:21 You shall call His name Jesus, for He will save His people from their sins. (KJV)

Acts 4:12 Salvation is found in no one else, for there is no other name under heaven given to men by which we must be saved.

Pentecost! What an amazing day that was when Fiery Tongues and Roaring Winds infused the apostles with the Holy Spirit so they could go out and proclaim the Gospel with power and authority! They preached a "Jesus" who had been Resurrected from the Dead, and in His name they were producing signs and wonders. A lame, blind beggarman called out to Peter and John, asking for money, as the two were going to the temple. Peter looked the man full in the face and said, "Silver or gold I do not have, but what I have I give you. In the name of Jesus Christ of Nazareth, walk." (Acts 3:6) As the beggar jumped and ran about, praising God, onlookers were filled with wonder at the power of the name of the Resurrected Jesus.

Those who had put Jesus to death were alarmed. Wanting to stamp out this fever that was spreading among the people, they ordered Peter and John to "speak no longer to anyone in this name" (Acts 4:17), which, of course, landed on deaf ears. The name of Jesus continues to be uttered from the lips of men down through the ages.

Other names have been honored and revered. Names of men who seemed to promise the eternal welfare of the souls of their followers. Buddha, Confucius, Gandhi, Brigham Young, Joseph Smith, Descartes, Calvin, Luther, the Pope— but none of these are names by which we can be saved. No other name above the earth, or under the earth is able to save us from our sins and make us right with God. Our source for this truth is the Holy Bible and on its Word we stand. Other names rise and fall on the tides of human events, but only One, Jesus Our Lord Emmanuel, has the power to save us.

In these modern days there are a myriad of names which may enthrall us— names of movie stars, athletes, political leaders, even family members and sweethearts, but we need to guard against any other name being above the name of Jesus in our hearts. After all, God "exalted him to the highest place, and gave him the *name* that is above every name, that at the *name* of *Jesus* every knee should bow, in heaven and on earth and under the earth, and every tongue confess that Jesus Christ is Lord, to the glory of God the Father." (Phil. 2: 9-11, emphasis is mine).

Prayer: Jesus, we bless Your Holy and beautiful name! Give us faith and courage to speak Your name to others. Thank You for dying for us, rising from the dead, ascending into heaven, and giving us the faith to believe in You. Hallelujah! Amen.

57

Tears in His Bottle

Ps. 56:8 You keep track of all my sorrows. You have collected all my tears in your bottle. You have recorded each one in your book. (NLT)

What a humongous sized bottle the Lord must have in which He collects all the tears from all the sufferings and sorrows of His people! Or perhaps there are many billions of individual bottles lining the shelves of heaven, and each labeled with the name of a hurting child of His.

Also, according to Psalm 56, there is a book in which God keeps a record of every teardrop shed.

Where do tears come from anyway– why are humans able to cry when many species are unable to produce them? Actually, being able to shed tears is a blessing for it helps us to release emotional tensions and stresses. A "good cry" is therapeutic for mind and body. There are two reasons that the lachrymal glands located behind the top eyelids are signaled by the brain to squirt forth salty water. One purpose is functional, i.e., to wash irritants from the eyes; the other is emotional, either to express joy or to wash sorrows from the heart.

My own mother went through a very sad era in her life when in the space of about four years she lost her husband, her mother, a son and a daughter. "I just can't cry anymore;" she mourned, "my tears have all been used up!" Surely tears would have helped to ease the heavy burden of loss that weighed upon her. Biologists explain that as we age the lachrymal glands often lose the ability to produce tears. However, the Lord was still cognizant of the tears that were shed within her heart, and He recorded those within His book.

Yes, God is aware of our suffering and He cares. One day there will be a full accounting.

The book of Revelation in the Bible explains that those who have come out of the great tribulation and have been washed in the blood of the Lamb will be sheltered and protected by God, and "...the Lamb at the center of the throne will be their shepherd; he will lead them to springs of living water. And God will wipe away every tear from their eyes." (Rev. 7:17)

Even now He wipes away tears. Do you remember when you were a child and skinned your knees? You ran sobbing to your mother who gently washed the blood from your wounds, applied a Band-Aid, and cradled you in her arms, wiping tears from your cheeks.

Likewise, your Father in heaven is attentive to your woes. When tears wet your pillow in the long hours of the night, turn to Him, and ask for His deep comfort and peace. Like a mother who welcomes a crying child into her arms any time of the night or day, He waits to comfort you, and He will tenderly collect your tears into His bottle.

Prayer: O Lamb of God, You walked this earth and wiped tears from Your eyes as You experienced suffering and sadness. O compassionate Lord, we bring You our tears, and rejoice in the comfort of Your Salvation. Amen.

58

Best Advice for Young People

Ecclesiastes 12: 1 & 12:6a Remember your Creator in the days of your youth...Remember him– before the silver cord is severed, and the golden bowl is broken.

What is the most important lesson you have learned in your life? What advice would you give to a young girl seeking answers to that question? Rachel Chandler was that inquiring girl who in the winter of 1993 sent out letters to a wide variety of famous persons seeking their opinions.

She aimed to use the acquired knowledge for a Girl Scouts project to earn a badge. She received many golden nuggets of wisdom which not only enriched her life, but eventually were included in a book, "The Most Important Lessons in Life: Letters to a Young Girl," by Rachel Chandler. (Guild America Books, an imprint of Doubleday Direct, Inc., Garden City, NY, 1997)

Taking time from their busy lives, notable people submitted to Rachel axioms...proverbs, for a happy and productive life. Mother Teresa wrote from India: "Be the sunshine of God's love." Barbara Bush encouraged Rachel by saying, "You have special talents and abilities, and you can make a difference for the better..."

One of my favorites was from Nancy Landon Kassebaum, a former U.S. Senator from Kansas, who urged Rachel to study hard and be ready to face the challenges in her future. She quoted Amelia Earhart, the famous aviator from Kansas: "Everyone has her own Atlantic to fly. Whatever you want very much to do, against the opposition of tradition, neighborhood opposition, and so-called common sense– that is an Atlantic."

Anne Perry, an author, expounded some sterling advice, "...I think to be able to love people is the most important of all. Never grow bitter or mean of heart. Never give up hope. Look for what is good, and you will find it."

Rachel's book is filled with many valuable guideposts for young people. But there is another Book, the Bible, which stands apart as a first resource for triumphant living. In it, people of all ages will find spiritual wisdom to help them make the most of their days on earth, "before the golden bowl is broken and the silver cord is cut."

"Come, my children, listen to me; I will teach you the fear of the Lord, whoever of you loves life and desires to see many good days..." (Ps. 34: 11&12) Listen to the Lord and learn of Him.

Prayer: Majestic Lord and Teacher, we pray for the young people. Supply them with strength to face the challenges of this corrupt and troubling world. May they "read, learn and inwardly digest Your Word" which will lead them to victorious living. Amen.

59

Be Not Ashamed

Matt. 10: 32-33 (Jesus said) Whoever acknowledges me before men, I will also acknowledge him before my Father in heaven. But whoever disowns me before men, I will disown him before my Father in heaven.

The definition of a "neologism" is "a newly coined word or phrase." "Tebowing" is one of those new words which has recently entered the vernacular of modern language. This interesting new coinage has now been recognized by the Global Language Monitor, which follows trends in language. "A news release from the Global Language Monitor's website says that the acceptance and use of the word 'has seldom been equaled.'" ("Lincoln Journal Star," Dec. 14, 2011) This website is deemed the "Webster's Dictionary" of the internet.

So what is one doing if he or she is "Tebowing"? The expression originated because an NFL football player, Tim Tebow, who is an ardent Christian, frequently takes a knee in prayer, bows his head over the knee, cupping one hand to his forehead, and holding the other hand aloft with a finger pointing heavenward in his athletic contests. This show of faith receives various reactions, ranging from high praise to criticism. A few sportscasters are rather snide when observing this habit displayed by Tim Tebow. They obviously do not approve of his overt Christianity. On the other hand, this young man, a remarkable athlete who formerly played for the Denver Broncos, now with the New York Jets, has been heralded by others for being a great role model.

Tim's parents have been missionaries to the Philippines for many years, and he grew up working with his family in spreading the Gospel. He gives all the credit and glory to God for his feats on the athletic field; and openly speaks of his faith, as a quarterback on the field when he encourages and prays with his team, and in interviews with the media.

Christians, including teenagers, are often mocked and ridiculed for speaking of their faith. One young man recounts being called a "Jesus Geek," or a "Jesus Freak" at school because he met at the flagpole for prayer with a group of young Christians, and was a leader in the Fellowship of Christian Athletes. Bullies are always looking for someone to pick on, and Christians are no exceptions as targets. Jesus never promised that it would be easy, but he did say in a portion of the Sermon on the Mount called the "Beatitudes": "Blessed are you when people insult you, persecute you and falsely say all kinds of evil against you because of me. Rejoice and be glad, because great is your reward in heaven..." (Matt. 5:11&12a) So, young people and old people alike, when bullies attack, confess with St. Paul, "I am not ashamed of the gospel, because it is the power of God for the salvation of everyone who believes..." (Romans : 1:16)

When bullies mock you, consider it an opportunity to practice your "tebowing." Take a knee, send up a prayer, and stay strong. Depending on the circumstances, it is not even necessary to take a knee; just send your prayer, and be glad for God's blessing.

Prayer: Dear Jesus, we bow before You, the Giver of Salvation. We give You the credit and the glory for our faith, and all the things You have allowed us to accomplish. Keep us safe and in Your care always! Amen.

60

30 Minutes Well Spent

Matt. 11:28 Come unto me, all ye that labour and are heavy laden, and I will give you rest. (KJV)

Fibromyalgia or chronic fatigue syndrome is a condition that plagues a friend of mine. It gives her much pain, including tenderness in the joints, muscles, tendons and soft tissues. As a wife and mother, she despairs of this affliction that slows her down and seeps away her energy. There are few antidotes, but one doctor has told my friend that it is vital for her to lie down for 30 minutes mid-day, everyday. And he said, "I mean lie flat on your back, not reclining in a chair!"

Surely, even for us who don't suffer from fibromyalgia, a 30 minute rest in the middle of the day would be helpful. To just lie quietly gives our immune systems a chance to recoup, and our minds and spirits a time to refuel.

"Think of what a better world it would be if we all-- the whole world had cookies and milk about 3 o'clock every afternoon and then lay down on our blankies for a nap," wrote Robert Fulgrum in his delightful best-seller, "Everything I Need to Know I Learned in Kindergarten." Indeed, the afternoon "siesta" or "quiet time" might be good for the population, adults as well as children.

One wonders, in truth, if some of the turmoil in the world would abate if everyone would "cool it" for a while each day, slow down the hectic pace and breathe deeply in a supine position. A 30 minute break would surely enhance our lives.

One hectic day when the apostles had become quite frazzled by inter-acting with the crowds, Jesus knowing their need for replenishment said, "Come with me by yourselves to a quiet place and get some rest." (Mark 6:31b)

If at all possible, let's take a 30 minute time-out today, come away with Jesus and rest on His everlasting arms.

Prayer: Dear Lord, please bless and help those who struggle with debilitating conditions. May they find rest and refreshment in You. Amen.

61

A Work in Progress

Phil. 3:12 I don't mean to say that I have already achieved these things or that I have already reached perfection. But I press on to possess that perfection for which Christ Jesus first possessed me. (NLT)

Even the apostle Paul who had many badges of merit in this faith-walk, declared that he was a "work in progress." Paul had come a long way, but he was the first to admit that God hadn't achieved perfection in him...that would not be fully accomplished until his entry into heaven.

Furthermore, Paul was confident that our Lord would not desert us, his projects, but keep laboring over us to bring us to completion on the last day. In Philippians 1:6 he wrote: "I am certain that God, who began the good work within you, will continue his work until it is finally finished on the day when Christ Jesus returns." (NLT)

Recently, some friends and I were discussing a renovation project on the main street of our hometown. "It seems to me that those large circular gardens which eventually will extend out into the intersection so intrusively on all four corners are going to interfere with the flow of traffic," I remarked.

"What's the matter– don't you like progress? I *like* progress!" one adamant lady admonished me.

This exchange made me stop and consider: Is *change* always *progress?* We live in a world that is constantly changing—but is it always for the better? Certainly, I would be one of the first to laud the progress of mankind that has produced the blessing of indoor plumbing and inoculations against many dread diseases. But the "progress" of landing a man on the moon, as amazing as it was, makes me wonder about its real value to humanity, especially considering the cost.

Throughout the ages, some people have resisted certain advancements such as electricity or motor cars which eventually became acceptable to most of society. (But one could find the thirst for oil inspired by the gasoline engine to be a questionable advancement in the long run.)

Surely all of us can agree that many developments can be used for good *or* evil. Consider television, drugs, guns, the printing press, the internet. Ah, Progress, what a fickle mistress you are!

But there is one kind of progress that is noble, uplifting, and of eternal value, and that is the progress the Holy Spirit makes in the faith-growth of God's children. And it's an on-going thing...we are a construction zone and there's a sign on our foreheads that reads: "Watch this site— something amazing is coming here!"

So to my friend's challenge, I answer, "Yes, I love progress, progress of the spirit... growth in the soul!" As St. Paul declared with certainty: God will continue His work in us until the day of Christ's return.

As to the outcome on our main street, it remains to be seen. As to the outcome of one who is trusting in Jesus, the answer is sure. You will turn out perfect!

Prayer: Gracious Construction Engineer of my soul, just as You have worked in all Your saints and apostles, continue Your work in me until that day of perfection in Jesus. Amen.

62

By His Hand

Ps. 95: 4&5 In his hand are the depths of the earth, and the mountain peaks belong to him. The sea is his, for he made it, and his hands formed the dry land.

One of the most marvelous of our Lord's creations is the human hand. Imagine a world in which we might have only possessed bear claws or duck wings. God equipped us with agile fingers and opposable thumbs which set us apart from the other species.

Twenty-nine bones, twenty-nine joints, an amazing amassment of nerves, blood vessels and sensory branches fulfil the commands of our brains. In fact, about one-quarter of the brain's motor cortex (which controls all movement in the body) is designated for the hands.

Hands– the finely-tuned tools by which we work and play, love and live are a gift. The Lord formed us with His mighty hands to be His hands while we are here on this earth. Many good works are performed by hands– works of surgery, nursing, fixing, building, feeding, operating, communicating, comforting, helping...the list is endless.

A very touching slide show which I once saw concerned "hands." As the song "He's Got the Whole World In His

Hands" was sung in the background, hands of people through-out all stages of life were shown, as well as all walks of life. From the plump little exploring hands of babies to the wrinkled and large-veined ones of oldsters, we were shown human hands in all their ways of being.

The Psalmist declared: "Your hands made me and formed me; give me understanding to learn your commands." (Ps. 119:73) Since His hands made us, we need to heed His desires and seek to understand how He wants us to use our hands to serve Him.

Our hands were made to bless others, and not to do evil. If we use our hands to sin and to do hurtful things against God and man we are urgently warned to change our ways in Mark 9:43: "If your hand causes you to sin, cut it off. It is better for you to enter life maimed than with two hands to go into hell, where the fire never goes out."

Our hands are ruled by our minds and hearts, and if we have good and holy thoughts, then our hands will follow with good works. Not that good works will save us, but that we are His children, drenched in His grace and mercy, and trusting Him for salvation. Then our minds can't help but put our hands to tasks that are pleasing in His sight. For it is written: "Who shall ascend into the hill of the Lord? Or who shall stand in his holy place? He that hath clean hands, and a pure heart." (Ps. 24:3-4a) (KJV)

Prayer: Our Creator Father, we are so grateful for the gift of our amazing hands. As we fold them now in prayer, please bless them to fulfil Your purposes and to be a blessing to others. Amen.

63

A Beautiful Mansion

John 14:2 In my Father's house are many rooms; if it were not so, I would have told you. I am going there to prepare a place for you.

Matt. 6:19-20 Do not store up for yourselves treasures on earth, where moth and rust destroy, and where thieves break in and steal. But store up for yourselves treasures in heaven, where moth and rust do not destroy, and where thieves do not break in and steal.

It is a beautiful mansion, pink stucco with high arched windows, porticos, and carved banisters marching up both sides of the double-entry stairs to the second level and all across the second story veranda– a Disneyland fairy tale palace– but in the coming months it will be burned to the ground. Yes, this elegant house near Gretna, NE, will go up in smoke and flames as a firefighter training site. Nothing will be spared, including the ten bathrooms, the sauna, the half-court basketball room with a twenty foot ceiling.

The mansion was built by former NFL star Rod Kush in 1997. His chain of small furniture stores fell on hard times, so he "downsized" to a smaller residence after living in the mansion only ten years. The property which includes thirty-five acres changed owners a few times after Kush sold it for $1.6 million. (It had cost him $2.6 million to build it in the first place and who knows how much more in taxes and upkeep in the short time the Kush family lived there.)

Somehow, standing water filled the vacant mansion and it became over-run with mold. One could not enter the building without wearing a mask. Vandals also broke in and did their share of destruction. It would cost more to clean up the house than it is worth so the developer who now owns the land has turned the demolition over to the Gretna fire department.

Aren't we who follow Christ the fortunate ones? Our mansion in heaven is being kept safe for us, and Jesus has gone there to prepare the rooms for us!

We do not need to worry about moth and thieves, mold and vandals. The mansion stands firm forever, and its beauty will surely take our breath away as we dwell there in the radiant glory of our Savior.

We spend so much time and energy on our earthly homes, but one day they, too, will crumble and fall. The leaky roof, the leaf-filled gutters, the peeling paint and wallpaper will no longer concern us...we are headed to a mansion, incorruptible and truly *beautiful!*

When we lay up treasure in heaven, when we are trusting in Jesus, we have invested in the best "house insurance" available. Our souls do not have to worry about wind or weather, vandals or vermin, and, most of all, becoming fodder for a demolition fire!

Prayer: Dear Father in Heaven, some people say that it was wasteful, even sinful, for Rod Kush to build his pink mansion. I leave that for You to judge; I just want You to keep me ever mindful of my mansion in heaven, and focused on gathering treasures to live there with You one day! Amen.

64

Calico Angel Wings

Hebrews 12:2 Let us fix our eyes on Jesus, the author and perfecter of our faith, who for the joy set before him endured the cross, scorning its shame, and sat down at the right hand of the throne of God. (NIV)

Blond hair cascaded from the top knot of First Angel, who was rehearsing busily for the Christmas pageant. In her white gown made from an old sheet by her mother, she was hopping about, arms spread-eagled, trying out her new cardboard wings.

The celestial bliss was soon interrupted though, as cardboard wings dangled from their perilous string attachment. Running to her mother, she mourned, "Mommy, my wings keep falling off!"

Oh, Lord, my heart echoed, *so do mine.* My saintly Christian angel wings keep falling off. So often I fail Him. So often I shed my wings in disobedience and selfishness. Sometimes I speak words that are unbecoming of a Christian. My mouth gets me into a lot of trouble, and I constantly feel my less-than-perfect wings slipping off.

At times I am slow to take thought of the disadvantaged in the world. I'm too wrapped up in my desires and obsessions. Sometimes my wings really are stiff cardboard wings that do not fly to do God's will. Too often, they are only ordinary calico wings, very unlike the splendid, holy wings that propel God's mighty angels. The writer of Hebrews tells me that I must keep my eyes on Jesus who is the *perfecter* of my faith.

Once in California there was a popular radio host, comedian, and song writer who enjoyed his womanizing, drinking, and party-boy life. Then a young pastor came to town and during one of his tent meetings, the radio host was convicted, and later went to that pastor's hotel room and asked what he could do to be saved. That night he got down on his knees and accepted Christ, and his life was turned around.

When a beer company was accepted as a sponsor of his radio show, he balked and ended up without his job. His professional life went into a slump, and he lost his popularity with the "In-crowd" of Hollywood.

Some time later, he ran into an old friend who asked what had caused such a change in the former radio host. To which, Carl Stuart Hamblen replied, "It's no secret. All things are possible with God."

"That sounds like a song title," replied the friend. Inspired, Hamblen sat down and wrote, "It is no secret what God can do...what He's done for others, He'll do for you. With arms wide open He'll pardon you..." In the 1950's, that song, the first cross-over gospel, country and pop ballad, topped the charts and was taken into the heart of the nation.

By the way, the young pastor was Billy Graham, and the friend was John Wayne.

So when our faith wings start drooping, it is no secret what we can do, just keep our eyes upon Jesus, the author and perfecter of our faith.

Prayer: Dear Lord Jesus, thank You for dying for us. Thank you for all You endured to provide us with forgiveness, joy, and peace. Help me through Your grace to keep my eyes steadily gazing upon You.

And also, Lord, that little girl in the pageant with the troubling wings, keep her going to Sunday School, learning about You, and ever growing in her faith. Amen.

65

The Price of an Education

Galatians 3:28 There is no longer Jew or Gentile, slave or free, male or female. For you are all one in Christ Jesus.

Some American kids take a free public education for granted, while there are other young people, especially girls, who yearn for the privilege of going to school. As a teacher I often heard students bemoaning the fact that they had to come to school. What an irony when others in the world are exposing themselves to great danger to do so!

Take fourteen-year-old Malala Yousafzai, for instance. In the fall of 2012, this young Pakistani girl was on a school bus in the Swat Valley. Members of the Taliban, a terrorist Muslim sect which does not believe in female education, climbed aboard a school bus, yelled for Malala by name, sighted her and shot her in the head with the bullet entering above her left eye, traveling down her jaw, and exiting her skull. As I write, Malala, a bright and beautiful young girl, clings to life in a hospital in England.

The Taliban had sought her out because, along with her father, a girls' school headmaster, she has been a bold and courageous spokesperson for female education. She wants to be a doctor some day. In a 2009 documentary film she hade said: "In the world, girls are going to school freely. And there is no fear. But in Swat, when we go to school, we are very afraid of Taliban. He will kill us. He will throw acid on our face. He can do anything."

Two centuries ago, St. Paul wrote to the Galatians explaining that in Christ there is no such thing as "male and female." Indeed, Jesus always treated women with respect and dignity, whereas the culture of the Jews at the time held them in low esteem, counting them no more than chattel or property.

It was revolutionary that He would speak to a besmirched Samaritan woman at the well. He had compassion on women such as the one caught in adultery and about to be stoned, or the widow of Nain whose son had died. He defended the woman who washed his feet in expensive oil and dried them with her hair.

Some of his best friends were women, such as Mary and Martha, sisters of Lazarus. He taught Mary who sat at His feet, just as He schooled His male disciples. He valued her enough to speak with her about spiritual matters, and He encouraged her sister Martha to also come and listen.

Many of His followers were females who gave Him financial support, offered the use of their homes and aided Him in His ministry. After His Resurrection, He first appeared to women and instructed them to go and tell the disciples.

Women's liberation from the stigmas of culture began with Jesus. Obviously, Jesus cares for the likes of Malala, as He cares about all the children of the world, male and female.

He values our souls, whoever we are!

Prayer: Dear Lord and Master, please heal Malala and help her achieve the education that she so desires. Through knowledge, and Your Word, enlightened minds are set free! Praise to You for the opportunities afforded through an education that we so often take for granted! Amen.

66

A Thousand Points of Light

John 8:12 Then spoke Jesus again to them, saying, I am the light of the world; he that follows me shall not walk in darkness, but shall have the light of life.

It was the last night of our two-week camping vacation. Our family had traveled through most of the states of the Northwest and was now heading toward Nebraska through the long, lonely stretches of Wyoming on 1-80. Anxious to get home and tired of setting up our tent, we had decided to drive all night. It was my turn at the wheel through the "graveyard hours." Pop music played on the radio while my husband snoozed beside me on the front seat, and our two boys, sardined in the back seat, were also sleeping peacefully.

The tedious miles benumbed my tired body and spirit. I turned off the annoying disc jockey, rolled down the window, and tried to stay awake. *Lord,* I prayed, *reveal some truth to me here on this dark highway, splitting the high plains of Wyoming. Show me something that will revive my senses and my soul!*

Just then, about 3 A.M., as the car mounted the crest of a long hill, God did it! He showed me something! There, spangling the night like a black velvet box of glittering jewels, were the lights of Cheyenne, Wyoming!

I gasped at the glory of it. Miles and miles of lights necklaced the city, as they winked and sparkled out of the nothingness of the night. *It's beautiful, Lord!* I exclaimed. The sight made me wonder what does the Lord think when He looks down upon this dark world. Surely the sin that has blighted and darkened it, saddens His Holy Heart.

But out of the darkness, when He spies Christians who are radiating the light of Jesus, it must fill Him with joy, with quadrillions more joy than when I feasted upon the lights of Cheyenne. *Lord, keep me shining brightly, walking close to Jesus.* What a privilege to have been ignited with the Light of Life, Jesus our Lord, saved by His incandescent, eternal Light.

How important it is to pass the Light on to many more souls so that God will rejoice with great exaltation as He views thousand thousand points of light, great galaxies of light, sparkling from the bowl of earth.

Prayer: Radiant Jesus, we bless and thank You that through Your great love and mercy, You have rescued us from the darkness and have become the Light of our lives. Forgive our sins, fuel our lamps, and help us to be beacons of light, leading others to You. Amen.

67

Watermelon Temptation

Hebrews 4:14-16 Therefore, since we have a great high priest who has gone through the the heavens, Jesus the Son of God, let us hold firmly to the faith we profess. For we do not have a high priest who is unable to sympathize with our weaknesses, but we have one who has been tempted in every way, just as we are— yet without sin. Let us then approach the throne of grace with confidence, so that we may receive mercy and find grace to help us in our time of need.

One of the best times of the year for me is late summer or early autumn when we head for the Barada Hills to partake of the watermelon harvest. The sandy, well-drained soil of the Missouri River bluffs and the Barada foothills engenders a watermelon heaven.

As we drive along the dusty gravel roads lined with sunflowers and tall weeds, my mouth begins to water. Already I can hear the melon split before the knife, and taste the juicy, crimson fruit.

Following rustic "Watermelons for Sale" signs that direct us over the wending roads, we arrive at last at our favorite watermelon farm where acres of vines crawl up the sandy hillsides. At the farm house, we are given sample slices, and even though warm, they are juicily delicious!

We bring the magic home with us, the magic of a "thump-ing-good" watermelon, the clover fragrance of a newly opened one, the crunch of sinking teeth into a scrumptious heart. What therapy! Does anyone ever have a care in the world with a piece of watermelon in hand?

Sometimes I can't understand what Eve found so tempting about a common old apple! Now if it had been a piece of wa-termelon, I, too, couldn't have resisted.

Seriously, I know that what happened in the garden of Eden wasn't all just about fruit; it was about disobeying God by succumbing to temptation. Temptation comes in many guises, often with various end results. I recently read about a lady who was ministering at a prison for women. When she heard those iron doors clank behind her group as they entered, she was struck with the thought that any of us could be only one bad decision away from imprisonment ourselves. Whether stealing forbidden fruit, or acting out of jealousy, anger, or greed, we may be in jeopardy of being locked up. Sin imprisons, whether behind bars or not, so we need help resisting it. Paul tells us in I Cor. 10:13, "No temptation has seized you except what is common to man. And God is faithful; he will not let you be tempted beyond what you can bear. But when you are tempt-ed, he will also provide a way out so you can stand up under it."

Aren't we fortunate that we have a wonderful High Priest who understands how the tentacles of temptation can be so pervasive! He came to live and die for us so that He could help us deal with the power of sin and temptation.

In the garden of Eden, Adam and Eve lost their innocence when they ate from the tree of the knowledge of good and evil. That "apple" must have been as seductive as a piece of sweet, juicy "watermelon".... the temptation to sin usually is.

IN JARS OF CLAY

Prayer: O Gracious Lord Jesus, thank you for delivering us from everlasting damnation by Your death on the cross. Protect us from the power of temptation and keep us from all evil. Amen.

68

The Green-Eyed Serpent

Genesis 37: 3&4 Now Israel (Jacob) loved Joseph, more than any of his other sons, because he had been born to him in his old age; and he made a richly ornamented robe for him.

One wonders what that special robe looked like that led to so much trouble in Jacob's family.

Often referred to as the "coat of many colors," it must have been a splendid article of clothing. (A footnote in the NIV translation indicates that the Hebrew descriptive word for the coat is uncertain, thus it has several interpretations. In the NIV the coat is described as "richly ornamented" instead of "many colored.")

Nonetheless, the special gift that Jacob bestowed on his favorite son aroused such hatred in the older brothers that they "could not speak a kind word to him (Joseph)." (Gen. 37:46) When the brothers conspired to kill him in the field one day, it was his brother Judah who suggested selling him as a slave, rescuing him from slaughter. The brothers took the gorgeous coat, soaked it in the blood of a goat, and took it back to Jacob, declaring that Joseph had surely been torn to pieces by a ferocious animal.

Even from the time of Adam and Eve, the "first" family, sibling jealousy has led to hatred, and hatred to murder. Cain was upset because God had accepted his brother Abel's offering, but did not look with favor upon Cain's offering. So "Cain said to his brother Abel, 'Let's go out to the field.' And while they were there Cain attacked his brother and killed him." (Gen. 4: 8&9)

In post-Biblical times, family jealousies and hatreds mar the canvas of history. One of my peers, a woman who had issues with her sister while they were growing up, now regrets her former emotions and attitudes. It seems her younger sister was beautiful and Lila was rather plain. Her younger sister, Jen, was a gifted and popular musician, homecoming queen, the whole nine yards. Whatsmore, Lila's parents spent a good deal of money on piano lessons and dance academy for her sister. Lila burned with resentment and would have little to do with Jen, who was five years her junior, even though Jen tried so hard to get close to Lila. Fast forward thirty years, finally the barriers have been broken down, and the two women have become best friends. "I *so* regret all the wasted years when I shunned my little sister," says Lila. "I missed out on a valuable relationship because of my jealousy!"

Ah, how that green-eyed serpent uses such emotions to wrap himself around hearts and destroy relationships! Jealousy and envy wreak havoc among families, and among nations. We need constant vigilance in prayer to subdue our baser emotions and heed Jesus's command to love one another as He has loved us. (John 13:34)

Lila would now be the first to admit that "A heart at peace gives life to the body, but envy rots the bones." (Proverbs 14:30)

Prayer: Dear Loving and Forgiving Father, help us to control our baser emotions which lead to hatreds, disruptions, and even death. Help us to love one another even as You have loved us. Amen.

69

The One for Whom We Live

I Cor. 8:6 ...yet for us there is but one God, the Father, from whom all things came and for whom we live; and there is but one Lord, Jesus Christ, through whom all things came and through whom we live.

When a man who was an expert in the law came to Jesus and asked how he could attain eternal life, Jesus responded, what does the law say? *"And he (the expert) answered, 'You shall love the Lord your God with all your heart, and all your soul and all your strength.... and your neighbor as yourself.'" (Luke 10:27)* And Jesus affirmed in so many words, "you've got it...that's it!"

But, oh, how hard it is! There are so many things that would divert our affections away from our Lord. Daily concerns and compelling passions steal our thoughts and our best intentions. Even our desire to serve Him can become the primary force of our lives in which we, as the old saying goes, "throw the baby out with the bath water." We can become so caught up in "church work" that we have little time for devotion and prayer. Contrary to our purpose, there is a danger of losing Him in our heaven-bent service.

We can also lose Him in the ups and downs of just being alive. Sometimes disaster drives us closer to the Lord, but sometimes it turns us against Him. To love Him with all our hearts means to love Him in good weather and in bad weather, in riches and poverty, in suffering and sunshine, in trials and in triumphs, in joy and in sorrow.

The apostle Paul resounds over and over again in his epistles that his all-encompassing desire was to know and love Jesus, to abide in Him and strive to be more like Him. In Philippians he wrote: "I consider everything a loss compared to the surpassing greatness of knowing Christ Jesus my Lord...." (Phil. 3:8a) In Philippians 1:21 he wrote, "For me to live is Christ and to die is gain." Paul's focus and the center of his life was always Jesus...Jesus...Jesus! Oh, that I could be as committed, as focused, as deeply in love with Him!

I am confident that on the last day when my time on earth shall end, all the secondary things will be lost in the draft as I am swept upward to meet Him in the skies. Then my focus will be utterly, completely on Jesus. May each day I am alive be preparation for that great day and may God enable my efforts.

Prayer: Dear Jesus, our Lord and Savior, how much you deserve our all-encompassing love. Help us in our puny human efforts to be filled with Your Spirit so that we may love You more fully and more truly. Amen.

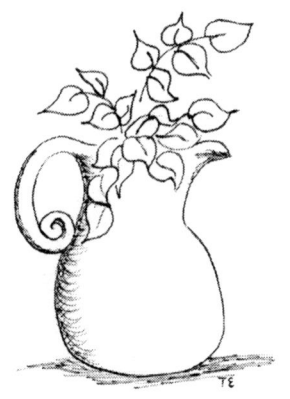

70

Royal Obligations

Luke 12:48b From everyone who has been given, much will be required...(NASB)

He stood in front of our class with rumpled clothes drawn over his paunchy belly as he took a piece of chalk and scrunched it across the blackboard, spelling out in huge letters, NOBLESSE OBLIGE. He turned to us, leaned his hands into the back of his chair, and asked, "What do those words mean?"

We were just some Kansas teenagers and none of us were acquainted with the French language from which this phrase arose, so we were stupefied. Mr. Jones, our venerable principal, just stood there peering over the top of his glasses with his penetrating blue eyes, demanding that we comprehend an important concept.

At last he said, "It translates 'nobility obliges' in English, so what do you think that means?" We shrugged our shoulders in silence. "Well, in former days it often applied to the landed gentry, royalty, or those of noble ancestry. These high-born individuals were expected to act in honorable ways, and to give back. Being noble means you have a responsibility to lead, to use your special talents, your gifts for the good of society. Each of you are nobility because of your education, your talents, your gifts, and opportunities in our free society. You each have an obligation to give back selflessly and honorably."

This memorable day in class has never been forgotten. In more recent years, I have learned that "Noblesse Oblige" has been adopted as the motto for the National Honor Society, and those teens are better acquainted with it than we were before that notable day in our rural high school over fifty years ago.

The phrase relates well to us as Christians. We are born of the highest nobility, children of the King, endowed with many gifts, expected to behave in honorable and selfless ways. We are obligated to the One who died for us, and rescued us from eternal death. "But you are a chosen people, a royal priesthood, a holy nation, a people belonging to God, that you may declare the praises of him who called you out of darkness into his wonderful light." (I Peter 2:9)

It is our obligation...and privilege!...to live out the nobility bestowed on us by God.

Prayer: Heavenly Father and King, Thank You for all the gifts I have been given as Your child. Help me to honor Your name, and use my gifts for the blessing of others. Amen.

71

Caught in Barbed Wire

I John I: 8&9 If we say that we have no sin, we deceive ourselves, and the truth is not in us. If we confess our sins, he is faithful and just to forgive us our sins, and to cleanse us from all unrighteousness. (KJV)

When I was a little farm girl I often had to walk a couple of miles to my one-room schoolhouse. The shortest route included crossing a barnyard, climbing through a barbed wire fence and then plodding across an expansive field. In the winter months when the field was full of snow, it was quite a challenge to navigate it in heavy rubber boots and bulky snow pants.

Returning home one afternoon, I lifted the top wire of the fence, bent over and put one leg over the lower wire. As I proceeded to pull the other leg through, I was startled to find that the barbs on the wire had caught in my woolen snow pants. I tried to go back through the fence, but couldn't! Neither could I go forward. It soon became apparent that I was trapped, and would not be able to free myself.

I yelled at the top of my lungs hoping to get my mother's attention, but she was sequestered within the walls of our stone house, and unable to hear my frantic calls. Cold and miserable, I dissolved into sobbing as the shadows began to lengthen across the field of snow.

Finally, my mother who was busy inside with my younger sister and brothers, noticed that I was not yet home. She put on her coat, scarf, and boots and came to investigate. What a relief when she pulled the barbed wire from my pants and set me free!

Sin is somewhat like that barbed wire that entraps us and holds us prisoner, grapple with it as we will. Benjamin Franklin wrestled with defects in his own character as he revealed in his autobiography in a section about "Arriving at Moral Perfection." He listed thirteen virtues he wished to perfect by charting them each day. If he failed at one of the attributes, he gave himself a black mark. Eventually, he admitted the impossibility of becoming perfect, but rationalized by saying in effect, "Oh, well, even if it were possible to conquer the traits, then I would probably have to struggle with the sin of pride at having been able to do so!"

Franklin's project reveals how limited we poor human beings are at achieving righteousness through our own strength. We can't perfectly keep the law (The Ten Commandments) and arrive at sinless and holy perfection, which is a terrible predicament for "the wages of sin is death..." (Romans 6:23a) And, no one is exempt for "all have sinned and fall short of the glory of God." (Romans 3:23) Try as we might there is only one way to be released from the grip of sin and that is by confessing our sins and accepting His forgiveness. "If we confess our sin, God is faithful and just to forgive us our sins and cleanse us from all unrighteousness." (I John 1:9 KJV)

We don't have to be caught forever in the barbed wire fence of sin. We can call to our loving Father who will release us, redeem us, and give us the gift of eternal life in Christ Jesus. (See Romans 6:23)

Prayer: O Holy God, I know that I fall short of purity, goodness, and righteousness. I confess and acknowledge my sins which are ever before me and ask You to save me from sin and death. Crown me with Your love and compassion today and always. Amen.

72

Send Forth the Choir

2 Chronicles 20:17 But you will not even need to fight. Take your positions; then stand and watch the Lord's victory. He is with you, O people of Judah and Jerusalem. Do not be afraid or discouraged. Go out against them tomorrow, for the Lord is with you. (NLT)

2 Chronicles 20:21 After consulting the people, the king appointed singers to walk ahead of the army, singing to the Lord and praising him for his holy splendor. This is what they sang: "Give thanks to the Lord, for his steadfast love endures forever." (NLT)

What if a commander of our army in Afghanistan gave an order that a choir should precede the forces as they marched into battle? And what if a battalion of singers really did lead the way, their colorful robes flapping in the breeze as they ascended a rocky mountainside, their joyful praises echoing from canyon to canyon? What a remarkable sight that would be!

But that, in essence, is what happened when Jehoshaphat was king of Judah in the 800's B.C. When the king was informed that vast armies of the Moabites and Ammonites were approaching Judah, Jehoshaphat sought the help of God. He proclaimed a fast for all of Judah. The people from every town came to Jerusalem for a summit meeting and Jehoshaphat stood in the courtyard of the temple beseeching the Lord, "We do not know what to do, but our eyes are upon you." (I Chron. 20:12)

Then the Spirit of the Lord spoke through a man named Jahaziel: "...the battle is not yours, but God's" (verse 15). "You will not have to fight this battle. Take up your positions; stand firm and see the deliverance the Lord will give you...Go to face them tomorrow, and the Lord will be with you" (verse 17).

Therefore, Jehoshaphat encouraged his troops, telling them to have faith in God and they would be successful. He then appointed men to lead the way to the battleground, singing songs of praise to the God who would deliver them.

Perhaps it was all that resounding music which confused the invading armies for they ended up attacking and destroying each other. When the Judeans arrived at the scene, they found dead bodies lying everywhere. They had not raised any weapon in the battle but their lilting songs! Joyfully, they returned to the temple, making music to God with harps and lutes and trumpets!

We, too, have battles to fight on this earth, and like good king Jehoshaphat we need to seek God in earnest prayer, and then march forth in faith with a song on our lips and in our hearts. For, indeed, God does inhabit the praises of His people. Wondrous things have been wrought through the power of praise! As we confront the many sinful forces which assail us daily, we need to put on our choir robes, tune up our voices with the strong chords of faith, and march forth, for the battle is not ours but the Lord's!

Prayer: Dear God, our Defender and Savior, You are splendid and holy, great and good! With full and thankful hearts, we give You the glory, and ask for Your help on this battleground called "Life." Amen.

73

Seeking Cotton Candy

Matt. 6:33 But seek first his kingdom and his righteousness, and all these things will be given to you as well.

When our youngest son was about six years old, our family traveled to see the Kansas City Royals play baseball. We were settled in the outfield bleachers when Son noticed a man carrying a large tray, blooming with big puffs of pink cotton candy, descending the stairs of an aisle a section away.

"Please, Mom, can I get some of that cotton candy," he begged.

"Not yet, look, George Brett is up to bat. You're going to miss what happens here!"

He was quiet for a while longer but I noticed he was more concerned about the retreating vendor than the action down on the emerald field in front of us.

After a while another bouquet of spun sugar came our way, lofted high on the shoulder of a man calling, "Cotton candy! Cotton candy! Only 50 cents!"

Again he begged to follow after the pink clouds. I gave him some coins and watched his blond head bob up and down the stairs, following his desire. After some time, he came back, waving his pink flag, and bearing a big grin. Before he knew it, the game was over. As we gathered up our belongings to leave, our pink-lipped youngster mourned, "Is it all over?" He had spent most of the time pursuing and eating cotton candy and had essentially missed out on the game.

Are we missing out as we seek to fulfil our lusts and longings in this narrow space called "life"? Some of us are on a never-ending quest for pleasure and we run headlong into movie houses and marinas, into casinos and sports arenas seeking fun and excitement. Some of us invade shopping malls, joining the throngs who seek to buy cars and clothes, gadgets and gizmos.

Seeking! Seeking! Whether it's a thirst for more knowledge, more power, a higher status, more prestige, or simply to meet our daily needs and provide for our families, we are as busy as a maze full of ants. But Jesus tells us that *first* we should seek God and His righteousness and He will take care of the rest. Certainly, many of the things we pursue will pale in importance as we seek more of God and His will.

In all of this, *time* is of the essence. Isaiah warned, "Seek the Lord while he may be found; call on him while he is near." (Is. 55:6) We must seek Him while the invitation is open and before our time runs out. Are we using all our energy and attention chasing after spun sugar, or are we seeking God and His righteousness? The ball game may soon be over!

Prayer: Our Father in Heaven, You are gracious, wonderful and patient. Draw us ever nearer to You, and may we seek Your face and Your Goodness over all else. Amen.

74

From the Stump of Jesse

Isaiah 11: 1&2 A shoot will come up from the stump of Jesse; from his roots a Branch will bear fruit. The Spirit of the Lord will rest on him— the Spirit of wisdom and understanding.

If you take a walk through the woodlands on a winter's day, you will see all around you the signs of death and decay. Gone are the green leaves of summer and the golden ones of autumn. They now lie shriveled brown and black under the trees which reach their bony arms into the gray skies of winter.

Fallen branches litter the ground, crunching in decay as we walk over them. Stumps of fallen trees are lifeless artifacts from nature's better days. One wonders if spring will ever be able to burst forth in bountiful growth from this barren landscape. And yet, experience tells us that the earth will once again flourish; that within seeds and pods, roots and stems, "there lives the dearest freshness deep down things,"* as expressed by Gerard Manley Hopkins, the English poet. How wondrous that within the mysterious realms of dormant nature, within trunk and stem, there lies the "dearest green."

The book of Isaiah uses symbolic language in prophesying the Messianic promise that would appear through the line of

King David. The stump– the root– of Jesse (who was the father of King David) would carry in its line some of the DNA of our Savior. This life-giving shoot from the decaying line of Jesse would provide hope for all mankind.

An old Christmas carol revels in this truth: "Lo, how a rose is growing, a bloom of finest grace; The prophets had foretold it: A branch of Jesse's race/ Would bear one perfect flow'r/ Here in the cold of winter/ and darkest midnight hour."**

In the depths of darkest winter, life was growing, "the dearest freshness" which sprang from the stump of Jesse. Praise God that the Rose of Sharon bloomed out of this world's depravity and sin, a lovely fragrant flower of redemption.

Paul echoed the prophecy of Isaiah in the New Testament and extended the Good News to us all: "The Root of Jesse will spring up, one who will arise to rule over the nations; the Gentiles will hope in him." (Romans 15:12)

Thank God for the gift of Jesus– the Messiah– born from the line of Jesse to plant eternity into our hearts.

Prayer: Oh, beautiful Rose of Sharon, Prince of Peace, King of the Nations, we come to worship at Your manger and adore You forever, world without end. Amen.

* From "God's Grandeur and Other Poems" by Gerard Manley Hopkins.

** From "Lo, How a Rose Is Growing", 15th century German carol, tr. By Gracia Grindal, b. 1943.

75

Windfall Dreams

Proverbs 11:28 Whoever trusts in his riches will fall, but the righteous will thrive like a green leaf.

"When my ship comes in, oh, the wonderful things I will buy!" Haven't we all heard words like that? Arlene Magdanz, a substitute teacher in the San Francisco Bay area, recently had her ship come in. Two wheelbarrows of gold coins were removed from the house of her deceased first cousin, Walter Samaszko Jr., a loner who lived in Carson City, Nevada. A cleaning crew that had been sent to clean out his house found the coins, more than $7.4 million worth, stashed away in ammunition boxes in his garage. After a search for heirs, a judge awarded the windfall fortune to Arlene. Nothing has been publicly stated by the recipient about her sudden wealth or what she plans to do with it.

One hopes that she will proceed with caution in managing this new-found money for research shows that four out of five people who win lotteries (which is a cousin to large inheritances) lose their fortunes and actually may end up in debt. They don't develop a personal mastery over their sudden wealth and miscalculate how to use it, squandering it recklessly. One lady from Florida even ended up spending over two years in prison for income tax fraud. (Her husband, who had assured her he was taking care of things, died of a heart attack during court proceedings and thereby escaped going to prison.)

Others went on shopping sprees, buying up to ten houses, giving away expensive cars to all the relatives, treating large groups of family and friends to lavish vacations. With sudden wealth, temptations seem to increase such as the use of drugs which trickles down to even children and grandchildren of the "lucky" winners. One man in West Virginia, whose whole family was devastated by drugs and death, wishes he had never won. Others report friction among members of the family and loss of friends, saying they were better off before the windfall, and wishing they had torn up their winning tickets. The prodigal son thought that an early dispensation of his inheritance would be his ticket to happiness. After taking his bundle and squandering it in wild, reckless living, he found himself penniless and hungry enough to wish he could eat the pods he was feeding to pigs in his minimum wage job. (Luke 15:11-16)

The Bible speaks often to the folly of trusting in riches (See the parable of the Rich Fool, Luke 12:13-21). Instead of selfish living we should share our wealth (The Rich Man and Lazarus, Luke 16:19-31) Proverbs 11:28 warns: "Whoever trusts in his riches will fall, but the righteous will thrive like a green leaf."

Yes, it is fun to dream of windfall riches, and even to plot how we would spend unlimited wealth. But we who trust in Jesus have already hit the jackpot! We have peace with God, forgiveness of sins and eternal life in heaven. With Jesus as our financial guide and advisor in all things, we will successfully navigate the waters of this earth, and ultimately receive the priceless gift of eternal life.

What mega-million windfall could ever compete with that?

Prayer: Lord Jesus, help us manage our money in ways that are in our best interests and will bring glory to You, whether it's a weekly paycheck, or a giant windfall! Amen.

76

For God's Pleasure

Eph. 1:5 His unchanging plan has always been to adopt us into his own family by bringing us to himself through Jesus Christ. And this gave him great pleasure.

Phil. 2:13 For God is working in you, giving you the desire and the power to do what pleases him.

Eric Liddell's sister, Jennie, once chastised him for missing a prayer meeting because of his running. He was a dedicated Christian, a missionary to China, a Scotsman born with swift feet and a desire to win, and perhaps his sister found that these things conflicted in Eric's life.

But he had found peace about his running, and he responded to Jennie with these memorable words: "I believe that God made me for a purpose. But He also made me fast, and when I run, I feel His pleasure."

The movie, "Chariots of Fire," related the vision of this famous runner, and his quest to join the Great Britain track team which would be participating in the 1924 Olympics in Paris.

He made the team but much to his dismay, later learned that the 100 meter race which was his specialty would be held on a Sunday. Remaining true to his Christian convictions, he refused to race on a Sunday. He made headlines around the world as he was both applauded and denigrated for his choice.

However, God had another plan for his runner. A teammate who had already won a silver medal in the 400 hurdles gave up his spot in the 400 meter race so that Eric, after all his hard work in training, would at least have an opportunity to participate in the Olympics.

The American coach, who was fielding athletes favored to win the 400, was dismissive of Liddell, decrying him as no threat to them. In a resounding and glorious victory, Eric ran the race of his life and won the gold medal!

Watching Eric win that race probably did bring great pleasure to God on that exhilarating day. But even more so, I believe He was especially pleased with the sacrifice Eric was willing to make for his faith and for his love of God, and God honored him for it.

And even so for you, dear brothers and sisters in Christ. God takes great pleasure when He beholds you using the gifts he has given you in special ways. Not only has He buried these attributes in us, but He has given us the desire to develop and use them, just as Eric Liddell did.

Perhaps we aren't as fleet as an Olympic athlete, but we have all been given various gifts which we can use to please Him. Whether it's singing, dancing, playing the violin, using a surgeon's scalpel, or cooking a fine meal, you may feel God's smile upon you as you refine your talents and offer them to Him.

But even more than these, God takes pleasure when we make choices which honor Him, when we demonstrate love for His people as Eric did when he went back to China after the Olympics to serve the people of China. That was the enduring sacrifice and the feat that fulfilled the great purpose of his life.

You may not be running down a white, sandy beach with the swelling music of Vangelis underneath you as in the stirring opening to the movie, "Chariots of Fire," but if you listen carefully, you may hear the great melodious heartbeat of God in the universe as He is pleasured by your particular gifts being developed and used to His service and to His glory.

Prayer: Oh, Loving God, how wonderfully You used your servant, Eric Liddell, and how Your power in him worked for Your pleasure. Give us also, that great longing to love and serve You. Amen.

77

He Has Your Back

Joshua 1:5b I will never leave you or forsake you.

Joshua 1:9b Be strong and courageous. Do not be terrified; do not be discouraged, for the Lord your God will be with you wherever you go.

While flipping through the channels recently, I came across an old movie entitled "Knight and Day," starring Tom Cruise as a secret agent who has an incredible knack for getting out of tight situations. His unwitting hostage, Cameron Diaz, screams through scenes in which he takes control of a pilotless airplane, single-handedly fights off whole armies of "bad guys" who are assaulting from all directions, or performs motorcycle stunts, including doing "wheelies" over the backs of stampeding bulls, with her holding on for dear life. With rakish confidence and a gleam in his eye, Knight keeps advising her, "Don't worry, I've got this!" In every death-defying situation, he repeats the refrain, "I've got this!"

Knight, a.k.a. Roy Miller, the hero of this action-packed movie, reminds me of Joshua, the Old Testament hero, who also had unflappable courage in some very difficult situations. He led the Israelites into the promised land and took on bands of giant-sized "bad guys." But in Joshua's case, his strength came from his faith and reliance on God's promise to him: "I will give you every place where you set your foot, as I promised Moses....No one will be able to stand up against you all the days of your life." (Joshua 1:3 and 1:5a) Thus God was essentially telling him, "I've got this! I have your back!"

Because Joshua believed God, he courageously invaded a hostile country and trusted the Lord to get him and his people through some harrowing and scary circumstances. We who live in New Testament days can relax for the promises of God are still in force. We may hold our breath as we hang from the helicopters of trials, problems, and desperate situations of all sorts, but that is when we need to hear again the reassurance from our Lord, the Master of the Universe,

"Don't worry! Relax in me! I am with you, and I'm in control of the situation."

Before He left the disciples in the last moments of His earthly life, Jesus assured them that He would send the Holy Spirit Who would be with them always. "If you love me, you will obey what I command. And I will ask the Father, and he will give you another Counselor to be with you forever– the Spirit of truth. The world cannot accept him, because it neither sees him nor knows him. But you know him, for he lives with you and will be in you. I will not leave you as orphans; I will come to you." (John 14:15-18)

The writer of Hebrews repeats the refrain first written in the book of Joshua: "Never will I leave you; never will I forsake you." (Hebrews 13:5b) So it behooves us to relax and trust in God as we take this often-times "wild ride" through life.

Prayer: We praise You, our Amazing God, that You "have our backs," and that You are with us always! Amen.

78

Waiting for the Dawn of a Better Day

Ps. 30:5 Weeping may last through the night, but joy comes with the morning. (NLT)

Surely there is no human alive on the planet who has not experienced dark nights of the soul. Among them was King David who wrote the Psalms. He was besieged by enemies on all sides, and continually called upon God for deliverance. He responded to God's faithfulness with songs of praise. For instance, he wrote: "But let all who take refuge in you rejoice; let them sing joyful praises forever. Spread your protection over them, that all who love your name may be filled with joy. For you bless the godly, O Lord; you surround them with your shield of love." (Ps. 5:11&12) (NLT)

Our enemies may not be the two-legged kind, but difficulties and griefs sometimes cloud our days with shadows and darkness. We cry out to God who may seem absent in our troubles, and we sometimes forget that behind the clouds His glorious light is still shining brightly.

In one particularly difficult season of my life, I barely slept two hours at a time as I tried to nurse my colicky newborn through the first two and a half months. My nerves became frazzled, and depression threatened to submerge my soul.

I had read that keeping prisoners awake by continuously dripping water on their foreheads was an ancient form of torture. Now I knew firsthand: lack of sleep is devastating to body and mind.

Outside our church one day, a kindly lady asked how I was doing, and all my pent-up stress came pouring forth in my response. She nodded compassionately, and gently said, "It will pass. It will pass." Just those simple words, and yet somehow relief washed over me. I believe that God spoke through my friend that day, encouraging me that things would get better.

And they did! Within days the baby started sleeping five and six hours at a time. Slowly my frayed nerves were mended, and I could take delight in my child instead of dragging through the days.

The dark night of my soul had passed, the clouds had parted, and joy had, indeed, come shining through with the morning. At last, I was able to see what had been hidden in shadows; God had been with me all the time, and He had carried me through the dark valley. I praise Him for His faithfulness in this trial, and in all others I have experienced in my life!

Prayer: Precious Lord, you surround us on all sides with the impenetrable shield of Your love. Thank You for being with us in the dark nights, and for bringing us through to joyful mornings! Amen.

79

The Christmas Truce

*Luke 2:14 Glory to God in the highest, and on earth peace to men on whom his favor rests. (The angels sang these words proclaiming **peace** on the night of Christ's birth.)*

John 14:27 Peace I leave with you; my peace I give you, not as the world giveth, give I unto you. Let not your heart be troubled, neither let it be afraid. (KJV)
(Jesus spoke these words shortly before he was put to death on the cross.)

France. 1914. World War I. A remarkable thing happened which rarely occurs in the theater of war. It had been a wet, cold, and miserable December. British and German soldiers on their respective sides were mired down in the mud of a large network of trenches separated by an open area called "No Man's Land." The trenches were only about 30 or 40 yards apart, close enough that the warring soldiers could call out and taunt each other.

On Christmas Eve, the British soldiers were surprised to see lights flickering on the rise of the German trenches. Decorated trees twinkled all along the front and then, lo and behold, they heard lusty voices singing "O Tannebaum." The British soldiers laid down their weapons and responded with "O Come All Ye Faithful." Across the divide, young German boys joined in the familiar carol, singing the Latin version, "Adeste Fideles." The singing of various songs continued until eventually, a board was raised up, and someone spoke, "I'm coming out; if you don't fire, we won't." Before long, muddied and battle-weary men met in "No Man's Land" with handshakes and greetings. Items from Christmas packages were exchanged, as well as cigarettes and souvenirs (even snipping buttons off their uniforms to exchange!) In one case, a soccer game broke out between the opposing forces which concluded when the ball was deflated by a barbed wire entanglement.

The unbelievable truce ended within days in most places along the line, but continued until New Year's Day in others. When they learned of it, the dismayed military commanders ordered that all such fraternizing with the enemy should not be tolerated. But it was too late for this particular Christmas in 1914 when young men saw each other, not as enemies but as brothers, and experienced a wonderful, if brief, "separate peace."

When Jesus was born in Bethlehem there was an eternal truce proclaimed by the angels between God and man. Formerly, our sins had put us at odds with God, and the fighting with God in our own souls made our lives miserable. There was no hope for us, but then an amazing thing happened: Jesus, the Lord's own son, was sent into the world to die on a cross, and pay for the sins which had separated us from Him. As it was written in Romans 5:1: "Therefore, since we have been justified through faith, we have peace with God through our Lord Jesus Christ..."

The vast "No Man's Land" of sin was breached when Jesus came to forge a peace between God and man. Meanwhile, on this earth, the fighting and wars never cease. The sins of anger, greed, prejudice, and hatred prevent us from seeing each other as brothers. The faces of our nations are scarred by the tools of war, and stained by the blood of conflict, and probably always will be until Jesus comes again.

The Christmas truce of 1914 lasted only a few brief days, but the justification made possible through Jesus Christ is a truce which will last throughout eternity. We only need to lay our weapons down, and come to Him, trusting and believing.

Prayer: Thank You, dear Prince of Peace, for rescuing us from the depths of sin, and giving us the faith to believe in You. Amen.

80

Thundering Hoof-Beats from Heaven

2 Thess. 1:6 God is just: He will pay back trouble to those who trouble you and give relief to you who are troubled, and to us as well. This will happen when the Lord Jesus is revealed from heaven in blazing fire with his powerful angels.

When I was a kid growing up on a Kansas farm, we didn't get to go to many movies. But during the summer months, the small town of Hamlin would show older films on a large white screen erected in an empty lot on the main street. Old wooden chairs were pulled out of the nearby city hall building for seating in this makeshift theater under the stars. An aging film projector was wound with large reels of celluloid "picture shows," and among our favorites were the "westerns" starring such heroes as Gene Autry or Roy Rogers. It was so exciting when these cowboys and their posses rode in to save the ranch, the town, or even the "girl"! The galloping hoof-beats of horses arriving in clouds of dust would elicit a rustle of "Yeahs" and clapping from an entranced audience sitting on a strip of grass, next to a gravel street, with fireflies winking in the wings.

There is something thrilling about the thunderous sound of racing horses, whether they are in the movies, racing around

IN JARS OF CLAY

a track, or over the hills of a ranch. That's why the image of Jesus riding in on a white horse in the book of Revelations fills my soul with awe. As described by St. John in Scripture revealed to him by God while he was exiled to the island of Patmos: In the final days, the heavens will part and "the Rider" will come upon a white horse, thundering through the skies with the white-robed armies of heaven following in His wake. (See Rev. 19:11-16)

This valiant Horseman will be "dressed in a robe dipped in blood, and his name is the Word of God." (Rev. 19:13) Out of his mouth "comes a sharp sword with which to strike down the nations." (Rev. 19:15) "On his robe and on his thigh he has the name written: KING OF KINGS AND LORD OF LORDS." (Rev. 19:16)

He will come as the All-Powerful Master of the universe, and he will come in judgment, Justice, and Truth. He will be welcomed by the glad shouts of the Faithful, and all others will tremble as they see "his eyes like blazing fire, and his head adorned with many crowns." (Rev. 19:12)

What magnificent imagery to portray the second advent of our Deliverer, Jesus Christ!

Signs of the end times are all around us in the world today. It is no fanciful movie plot– the Words of God are sure– Jesus will return again! Oh, listen...do you not hear the far-off hoof-beats even now as they are approaching, approaching ever nearer from the realms of heaven?

Prayer: O Powerful God, Just and True, I pray that when You come again, I will be found faithful, and among those who will greet You with loud hosannas. O, Lord, prepare our hearts for Your soon arrival. Amen.

CPSIA information can be obtained
at www.ICGtesting.com
Printed in the USA
FFOW04n1206221014
8250FF